!

Stupid!

Stupid!

A dog's life on war-torn Malta

BY

BERNARD DENVER

Bernard John Patrick Denver
1 May 2017

ISBN-13:9751546850878
ISBN-10:1546850872

Introduction

Stupid is a Maltese Terrier, he tells the story of Malta during WWII. The story starts immediately before the war and goes through to the end of the great siege in1943.

It is a story of survival. How Stupid (yes that really was his name) lived through the biggest blitz on earth. Malta received more tonnes of bombs in the month of April 1942 (6728 tonnes), than any other place on earth.

Secret work took his human Dad away from Malta in 1943. All communication with Dad ceased. After the siege, Stupid comes to Great Britain by convoy in 1943. Arriving in Liverpool after a hazardous voyage and then travelling north to live in Scotland. Eventually moving to England.

Where was his Dad and what was he doing? You'll have to read the book.

CHAPTER 1

Malta 4th of August 1939

I was born on this day along with two sisters and a brother.

All I can remember during those first few weeks was Mum carrying me from where I had wandered back to the safety of my family. This seemed to happen quite a lot.

I do remember Mum saying, 'you are a clever little boy, always wandering and looking for new adventures'. I think both she and I regarded this as being a good thing, although my sisters and brother had a different view. They were always saying, 'you'll get into trouble one day, just you wait and see.'

Perhaps I should explain a bit about myself. I am a Maltese Terrier who right from birth was always getting into trouble.

It was during one of my exploring walks that I really did get into trouble.

Malta has many steep passageways and steps. Anyway I thought, easy peasy, I'll just hop down a few steps and see what is round the corner. Just hopping down was easy, I was still quite small you see and the hop down proved to be just that a hop down but no hop up would work. So there I was stuck, no amount of shouting made any difference, boy was I in trouble.

Then out of the blue came a big hand, which said, 'now then young fellow, that was a stupid thing to do. Where is your family. I think your Mother is calling let's go and see'.

Mum was really angry, I think for two reasons, one for wandering off and the other because she didn't find me before the big hand found me. She was so grateful to the big hand, she said to it, 'perhaps you may want a dog of your own one day, this little one will be old enough to be on his own soon, perhaps just perhaps you will call again'. Of course the big hand didn't understand a word what Mum said, not many big hands do you know.

However the big hand must have realised a bit of what my Mum was saying because it spent a long time stroking her and soft sounding words were coming from somewhere up high.

My sisters and brother were most upset and they kept on saying again and again, 'that was a really stupid thing to do, really, really stupid'.

It wasn't long after the big hand found me that I felt it was time to join the big world I knew was there. My wanderings had helped me to be ready before my brother and sisters.

One day the big hand returned only this time there was a little hand with it. Mum was very excited about the return of the big hand with the soft and gentle voice and now there was another voice which was just as pleasing.

'We have come to look at the little fellow I met on the steps', said the big hand. The little hand said, 'my husband has told me so much about this little fellow we just had to see him'.

Mum was so pleased, she kept on saying that this was just what she had hoped for. Of course the big and little hand did not understand a word that Mum said. Not that it mattered it was quite obvious to the whole wide world what she was saying.

Mum called me over, 'now these two kind people have come here and I am sure they will want you to go with them, and if you decide to go that is, they will become your Mum and Dad'.

People, they are people, I thought to myself and not just big and little hand. Well now let me have a good look at these people. I was only just learning about humans and as far as I could see they looked alright to me.

Mum looked at the two humans and then at me. They realised what she was saying. 'So now what is your name', said the little hand. 'When I found him', said the big hand, 'most people would have said he was doing something stupid. However in my view he is a highly intelligent creature looking for new adventures'. 'Quite right', said my Mum, humans would call it a bark. Little hand went quiet for some time and then said, 'so the world thinks he is stupid and we know he is highly intelligent then the answer to his name is Stupid. That will teach the world never to judge any creature or human by name'.

So you see that's how I got my name.

CHAPTER 2

A New Home

The big hand lifted me up and tucked me under his arm. Perhaps from now on I should be saying my Mum and Dad took me home. As we went along for the first time I noticed many humans walking in and out of buildings and then there were other animals pulling things with stuff on them. It wasn't long before we came to a building with two steps leading to a door. Dad used what I now know is a key to open this door and in we went. Dad said, 'now then Stupid this is your new home and your Mum and I hope you will be very happy here.'

Well it certainly felt good and I could see a water bowl for me which reminded me that the walk home took a few minutes and I needed the toilet quickly. The stone floors seemed just the place. Mum noticed immediately what I was about to do. She picked me up and rushed me to another door for a good reason.

I soon learnt how to behave in this new world and I must say I was enjoying it very much especially when I was allowed to sleep on the bed with Mum and Dad.

Every morning Dad used to get dressed in what Mum said was his uniform and off he used to go somewhere, going on duty, Mum said. Every day he came home and put on what Mum called his civvies. This became an exciting time for me because it meant we all went out for a walk with me learning how to be on the end of a lead.

Shopping seemed to be a favourite thing to do for Mum although Dad always went quiet whilst Mum went around the shops buying food, some of which was for me. She said Dad got fed up pretty quickly with this exercise because he was missing his afternoon game of Hockey. I know this because she used to say things like, 'well you have to give it up some time, you now have a family,' I barked, that must be me, and there's a war on you know.

What this thing called a war was I didn't know, it was something everybody we met kept on talking about. Just like shopping Dad was pretty fed up with all this talk about war. He said to Mum that there was every chance a man named Mussolini would declare war on Britain shortly and that meant Malta would be in line for trouble.

Mum understood why Dad was fed up. I heard

her telling a friend that Dad's 21 years in the army
were up in 1940, which was now and that we
were supposed to be going to America to join his
brothers in a place called New York.

Unfortunately the army said he could not
leave Malta as there were no more ships to take
us anywhere. That meant wee jock, as the army
people called him, was on Malta for what they
called the duration.

For me this was a good time, as each month
went by I was given more and more freedom to
roam wherever I wanted. I followed Dad to where
he worked overlooking the Dockyard. He was
a Royal Engineer and like all Engineers he had
to perform many tasks in making sure all the
equipment he was responsible for was kept in good
working order for harbour defence.

At first Dad didn't like me following him to
work, however all military and civilian personnel
liked me hanging around watching them work
and if I went missing when helping Mum with the
shopping they would shout out the next day Stupid
is back and I got extra tit bits.

I suppose being a dog I picked up a change in
atmosphere quicker than humans. Each day I
heard the humans talking about how things were
in Britain and how this war was not going our way
at all.

Mum, Dad and I were still having fun every day. We used to have great walks all over the Island. Sometimes we went by bus before being dropped off at strange sounding places and then walking back home for tea.

I remember Dad talking about leaving Mum in Britain some years ago when he was suddenly posted to a place called Egypt. He was there for a year doing something with underground cables on the Libyan/Egyptian border.

Dad said he knew that one day there is going to be trouble with this person called Mussolini who ruled Libya.

Meanwhile Mum left in Britain had no word from Dad and so she went to her home which was Gibraltar. All her friends and family said to her, there you are, you see we told you not to marry a soldier, you will never see him again. Mum was not in the slightest bit worried, she knew Dad would never let her down their love would last forever. After waiting for almost one year she suddenly received a letter, come to Malta right away, I have a great present for you. Mum's sister read this letter to her.

Now, you might find it very strange that I, a Maltese Terrier called Stupid can write a book such as this. And you might also find it strange that one of the most intelligent women ever on this earth cannot read or write, that person being my Mum. Well all I can say is read on because most of what I write is true, not all of course just most.

Mum soon found a ship that would take her to Malta. She said it was a Japanese ship. She liked very much as it was spotlessly clean. Of course when she met Dad you can imagine how wonderful it was for both of them. They were so happy to be together again. As you know Dad was still very much in the army and it was the army that offered what is called married quarters to live in. However they decided that was not for them and they were lucky to find a house to rent near where I was born in a place called Floriana. The house was where in years gone by, the Admiral used to live. As you can imagine it was quite high up overlooking the Grand Harbour.

CHAPTER 3

The War is coming

As soon as Mum had unpacked her things she quickly came to the subject of the present. You know the one dad had promised in his letter about coming to Malta. She was so excited and so she had a few guesses. There was only one problem there was some silly bird making noises in a room somewhere and it was distracting her from thinking about the present. Anyway she had a go, was it a bracelet, no, was it a necklace, no, was it earrings, no, was it a ring, no, well what is it. Dad went into the next room and appeared with a cage and in it was that bird, yes the one making all the noise.

Mum saw the funny side of this present, in fact she spoke about it for many years to come. It was a wonderful story and everybody that heard the story couldn't help but have a laugh.

Life continued in much the same way as when I first arrived at the Admiral's house in Floriana. We were all very happy and enjoying life to the full.

It became noticeable that Dad was spending

more and more time on duty. He said it was because he had to make sure all his equipment for harbour defence was in good working order. Everybody we met on our walks spoke more and more about this thing called war. They said we were losing to a man called Hitler. They also said the man that Dad spoke about a few months ago, his name was Mussolini, was going to join with Hitler. As Mussolini lived in a place called Italy which was close to Malta it could only mean trouble for us in Malta.

As we know Dad had spent a year in Egypt beside the Libyan border before being posted to Malta. Libya was part of the Italian Empire. He just knew that one day we would have to face Mussolini. He wanted us out of Malta altogether. He said it was his sea that Malta was in and no British person should be there.

It was now the 10th June 1940 and Mussolini declared war on France and Great Britain. As you may have gathered this was no great surprise to my Dad.

For the first few days after that date Dad and I walked to and from the harbour as usual and of course Mum went shopping.

At first the Maltese people did not pay too much attention to the war declaration, simply because they thought the Italians would not bomb and invade a fellow Roman Catholic country. Within a few days they realised that this was a false hope. In fact as soon as the Italian air force appeared over Malta, the Maltese lashed out against Mussolini and not only that, they even laid the blame on the head of the Roman Catholic Church, the Pope.

Being that I was only a dog and that Mum and Dad didn't seem too worried about the war, neither was I. In fact Mum used to watch the Italian planes flying high over the harbour, supposedly trying to bomb us. I used to sit with her and watch the planes come towards the harbour and then turn away as soon as the guns started shooting at them. We often used to see three little black dots moving in and out of the Italian planes and occasionally we could hear a ratatatat of guns from the planes.

The three little planes, Dad told Mum, were called Faith, Hope And Charity and they were our only air defence against many Italian planes. Sometimes the Italians did manage to bomb Valetta, which was where Dad had his workshop. Every time a raid was due, the siren sounded and Mum and I went underground to the air raid shelters. Dad's main job was to keep the searchlights working for the night raids. The cables to operate the searchlights were often cut by the bombs and this meant working day and night. He also had to defuse any unexploded bombs before they were moved to be exploded later, well away from Valetta. Dad told Mum that some of the Italian planes that had crashed were very similar to our Gladiator aircraft, Faith, Hope and Charity.

Mum and I were coping quite well, living more and more underground. Food wasn't so plentiful, it was just enough. Water was a problem and Mum was constantly boiling and using a chemical to keep it clean.

Total War

January 1941 saw a complete change in just about everything in our daily lives. The bombings increased drastically, there were many more aircraft flying day and night, bombing and shooting everything. Malta was now under siege with the whole island being attacked.

These planes were not Italian, they were flown by a different type of person, one who was determined to kill us all. Dad said they were German and they came from a man called Hitler.

As each month went by food became harder to get. Mum and Dad were getting thinner every day. The ships that brought us food were not getting through. Even though we had more planes to fight with, it wasn't enough.

I noticed that my doggy friends were getting scarce. I often wondered if my own family were alive. Perhaps they were dead, like so many other animals and of course humans. I never heard

Dad of Mum talk about them ever again. Mum was getting worried about losing me, she always kept me very close to her when in the air raid shelter. I did notice that people were looking at me strangely with a hungry look in their eyes. It didn't worry me a bit I was very quick and I used to run to where Dad was in his workshop with Guiseppe. He was a Maltese civilian who came from a country area. They were firm friends and they worked together everyday. Once Dad got used to me going backwards and forwards from him to Mum he stopped worrying about me. I guess he knew my chances of survival were as good as any other animal or human. In any event Guiseppe and all the troops liked me there, I could tell by all the titbits I got. It was no wonder I didn't lose much weight.

Every day and night the air raids became heavier, so much so that Dad and I had to climb over more and more rubble every day. The months went by very quickly, in the end it seemed like one endless air raid.

Suddenly one day in July, Dad changed, looking far more worried than normal. He started talking to me about food. It was a different attitude in the way he mentioned food. Everybody talked about food, simply because there was none or very little anyway.

I tried to comfort Dad by having extra cuddles during the air raids. It was no use and then one day he whispered in my ear, I think you are going to have a baby brother or sister. Are you sure, I mean here we are a little family just surviving with hardly any food, with Mum looking thinner every day, I mean are you sure. We just looked at each other for a very long time. Yes, he was sure. Suddenly Mum wanted chocolate and lots of it quickly or we will be for it.

Whenever a submarine or a ship managed to get into harbour Dad and I used to go and look for food. I am very good at finding food especially chocolate, I can smell it a mile away. Chocolate in wartime is slightly more valuable than gold dust. It was my job to walk along side Dad and warn him when I smelled chocolate on a sailor, soldier or airman. Dad knew that any ship or submarine that managed to get into the harbour would have onboard troops who would have some chocolate on them. Mum was desperate for chocolate and so we were ordered to find some, or else. The thought of anything happening to Mum drove us on to finding chocolate. After all, this will probably be the saving grace for Mum and the baby.

Dad and I would go for walks around the

harbour paying attention for any troops who looked fit and well, with fairly neat uniforms. They were the ones most likely to have just disembarked from a ship or submarine. I went on ahead of Dad. Once I could smell chocolate on anybody, a few barks and a jump or two told Dad that this person had chocolate on them somewhere. In fact I knew where the chocolate was on the person. I never could get Dad to understand where it was. In any event it did not matter too much because everybody could see that Dad was a very thin small Royal Engineer. This meant he knew everything a new soldier, sailor or airman wanted to know. He couldn't be anything else other than a local soldier. All that Dad needed to do was ask if they knew where they wanted to go. Nobody ever did, so as Dad explained how to get to their destination, I would jump around the area where the chocolate was in their uniform. Of course Dad always just happened to mention that Mum was pregnant and guess what, the one thing she wanted to stay alive was chocolate.

Who could resist such a plea. Well nobody, well hardly anybody anyway.

All the ones that refused, I made a note of their smell, you never know it may come in useful later. It wasn't so much them refusing to give anything, after all they may have a starving friend or a

relative back at a shelter or wherever. No it was
how many simply lied they hadn't any. They were
good at it as well. I knew they did have chocolate
on them, they could be hoarders, perhaps a bit of
extra persuasion later on will do the trick. There
was this one chap who lied about not having
any chocolate on him. He wasn't exactly fat,
nevertheless he had a belly on him, which meant
there was no shortage of food where he came from
and as I said he lied, so I bit him on the ankle.
He went hopping mad and said to Dad, 'did you
see that, your dog bit me on the ankle.' 'Don't be
stupid,' said Dad, 'I didn't see anything, anyway
there's no blood running into your boot is there.'
'Don't be stupid, did you say, don't be stupid well
I'm not stupid.' 'No,' said Dad, 'my dog is Stupid,
except of course he's not.' The man was totally
perplexed and stood there scratching his head. 'I'll
get your dog one day,' said the man. That's what
you think chum, I said to myself. Dad and I went
along the waterfront laughing all the way.

I can remember a time when the air raids eased
off quite a bit. Dad told Mum it was because the
German air force based in Sicily had moved to
somewhere called Russia.

Something must have happened in Russia
because by January 1942 they were back and
this time they meant business. The raids became

bigger and bigger and they were without stopping all day and all night.

One day after making sure Mum was okay in the shelter, I went to see Dad at work repairing cables. There was a heavy raid on and I had quite a job climbing over new rubble to get to him. He was just pouring a cup of tea, when I arrived. Dad usually shared his tea with me and I was just going to have my first gulp when boom! A bomb went off fairly close. We looked over the wall where we were sheltering and Dad said, 'well there goes my workshop and Guiseppe with it.' By this time in the war all humans were shell shocked, which included, I might say us animals. Dad's reaction to this awful tragedy was just nothing, just nothing. I looked into his eyes he didn't see me. His eyes looked straight ahead they did not blink, they just looked and looked and looked. 'Come on, we have to find the pieces.' And so we slowly climbed over the wall to the road leading to where the workshop once stood. There was new rubble everywhere. We stumbled on a few steps and then stopped. There was a man walking towards us, a black man. Of course Dad knew what black men looked like, he lived in South Africa as a boy. However there were none near us in Malta at that time, many did come later. So who was this man, one thing for sure he didn't have any clothes on, not a stitch.

'It's Guiseppe!' Shouted Dad. I couldn't tell if it was or it wasn't; it wasn't his smell it was just an awful smell from a very wobbly black man. People came to help, Guiseppe couldn't speak, he just looked in the same way that Dad had a few minutes a go. Guiseppe was taken to hospital. It was amazing how quickly he recovered and within two weeks he was working again with Dad, although some of the black bits took a long time before they disappeared.

It was March 1942 and Mum said it was getting near the time when the baby was due. Dad said I was to take extra care of Mum and that I had to stay with her all the time until something happened. Something, what something. Dad looked at me knowing I didn't really understand. 'Not to worry Stupid, Mum will tell you to fetch me when the something happens.' Sure enough after a few days Mum looked decidedly strange, she seemed in pain. 'Go fetch Dad quickly,' she said. As usual there was a raid on, luckily a few miles away, so it was easy to get Dad and back we raced to Mum. Before we left the gun emplacements where Dad was working he had phoned for a taxi so that when we reached home it was waiting for us.

I guess Mum knew what Dad was going to say because she did not blink an eyelid when he said that he couldn't go with her to the hospital. So it was Mum and me and of course the taxi driver. 'Do not worry Mum, everything will be okay and Stupid will look after you.' 'I know,' said Mum.

Our journey from Floriana to Imtarfa military hospital would take some time with all the new rubble everywhere and there was always the chance of unexploded bombs to hold us up. To start with we were lucky and we managed to progress fairly well until about 2 miles from the hospital when a heavy raid started. The taxi stopped. 'That is it Missus,' said the driver. 'What do you mean that is it. You don't think I'm going on through this raid do you.' 'Get out.' With that the driver pulled Mum, me and the little suitcase she was carrying out of the taxi and drove off.

'Well, Stupid it's just you me and this little person in my tummy to get to the hospital.' Isn't Mum amazing, she just was so determined to get there and nothing was going to stop her. We saw nobody on our walk, everybody was sheltering. The noise was terrific, bombs falling all around us, we stumbled on with Mum holding on to her little case and me walking in front, showing the way. The raid eased a bit, it was quite obvious they were bombing Takali airport, which was right beside the hospital. It wouldn't be long before they would be back after assessing the damage and then it would

27

begin all over again. You see they used the hospital and its big red cross painted on the ground for aiming at the airport. It did not matter to them if a few bombs went and hit the hospital even though there were a number of their own aircrew in there, who were rescued after being shot down.

At last we could see the hospital, someone must see us, soon we could hear voices coming our way. There were three Nurses, two got hold of Mum and one took the suitcase. We entered the hospital and went up to the first floor. Luckily there wasn't too much damage in the area where Mum was put. 'Now then fellow me lad,' it was one of the Nurses, 'we cannot have any dogs here, whilst a baby is being born.' Mum said that if it was not for me she wouldn't have got there. Then she said to me, 'go to Dad and tell him I am okay. Ask him to come as soon as possible.'

Easier said than done, there was another raid starting and it was miles to go. I set off with a mind to watch out for people, they were all starving and one little dog would make a nice meal. It was evening and I decided to wait until it was dark before making a move. Not that it ever was really dark, with the raids continuing, the constant flashing of the anti aircraft guns, the bombs going off and the searchlights. I thought of Dad desperately trying to keep those searchlights going and all the while thinking of Mum. I must get through, I must try to keep on going through the night and with a bit of luck I will not get hit by any shrapnel. Worst of all was the parachute bomb. They were designed to explode before they hit the ground, so that people and buildings were obliterated. You see that Malta is made of limestone and when an ordinary bomb hit it penetrated the ground and sent most of the blast upwards. That's what Dad said anyway. He also said he never saw a Jerry plane go through the box barrage, protecting the harbour, without getting hit some where. What was this thing called a box barrage. From what I could understand it was all the guns concentrating their fire in a certain area together.

———————————

Poor Dad he must be worried sick about Mum and poor Mum what must she be thinking. I do hope the little one will be all right. All these thoughts were going through my mind as I threaded my way through the rubble. Every now and again I came across a clear patch and I raced along, keeping an eye open for any people. Boy was I getting thirsty and very hungry. Oh no! There go the sirens again and here come some people heading for the air raid shelter. Now let me see, those people came from over there and they were in such a hurry, I wonder. I came closer to where they came from and yes I can smell food and where there is food there will be water. If I jump on the boxes they were using as a table and drink the water, now for the food, scatter the dishes around and hey presto, they will think it bomb damage. Now I can complete my journey with a full belly.

I felt like a new dog, a few barks of happiness will not do any harm, nobody will hear me anyway, not with all this racket going on. I raced on running up and down piles of rubble. As I got nearer to Valetta the noise of the guns became intense and worst of all so did the shrapnel. It fell everywhere all sizzling and hot, it was only my small size that saved me. Every now and again the firing would die down and I could hear voices saying is that the end of the raid. They must be air raid wardens listening for the all clear. I heard one of them say, did you see that? See what, the other voice said. I saw something moving fast in the direction of Valetta. Get away with you, the bombs are driving you nuts, said the other voice. It was me of course on my way to get Dad.

It was beginning to get light and the raid had at last eased, that meant more danger for me, I had to be very careful and not be seen until I reached near where I expected to find Dad. I crept along to where the workshop once stood and listened.

There was nothing. Smoke drifted up from what
was left of a gun emplacement. Where were the
men, had they all been blown to bits. I did not
know what to do, so I sat down and listened once
again. Again nothing and so I barked and I barked.
Suddenly there was Guiseppe beckoning me to
follow. We went through and down some steps
cut into the rock. The steps went down in a spiral
and at the bottom it opened up into a big room
with chairs and desks scattered around. There was
Dad he was talking on the telephone to someone
and ordering something. I then noticed various
telephones around the room, all were being used.
As soon as Dad had finished talking I rushed over
to him and jumped straight into his arms. I was so
excited I think my tail nearly dropped off.

'There, there little fellow,' comforted Dad, 'let
me put you down and see what's to do. Judging
by the way you are acting Mum got there safely.' I
started to jump and run to the bottom of the stairs,
barking all the time.

'Guiseppe you stay here until they send a
replacement for me, show him the ropes, I will
be back as soon as I know Mum and the child
are well. Come on Stupid, we have to tell the CO
where we are going first and why.' We set off and
went to tell the CO. He was expecting to hear
about Mum and the baby and wished us well in

the hope that everything will be okay. Next we had
to get a few things together for Mum, the baby,
Dad and of course me.

How to get there in a hurry was the problem.
No use looking for a civilian transport, it had to
be military and with a few personnel on board
who will help clear the way of rubble. There was
every chance another raid would start soon. We
had to get away from Floriana quickly. As soon as
we reached the main road we walked and walked
until there was the sound of a truck approaching
rapidly. Dad stood still in the middle of the road.
The truck was not going to stop, it swerved one
way then the other when it saw me and stopped. A
loud voice was shouting what do you think you are
doing. There were voices in the back complaining
about being knocked around. Once Dad had
explained that he wanted to get to Imtarfa and
why; suddenly everything changed. They were
replacement crew for some anti aircraft guns on
another part of the island. They could take us
some of the way but that was all. We sat in the cab
and I sat next to the driver.

'Nice little fellow isn't he,' it was the driver
talking. Dad smiled. I could smell chocolate, I
looked at Dad, he was watching me, I looked at
the pocket where it was, then I looked at Dad.
'Do you know,' began Dad, 'that all the while my

32

wife was pregnant the one thing she wanted was chocolate, which of course is more difficult to find than gold dust.' The driver did a sort of swerve and his hand went to the pocket. 'Really well I never,' he said. We slowed and came to a stop, 'come on you lot, if you don't want to get blown to bits get out and move that rubble.' Off we went again until we reached a cross roads. 'This is where we have to leave you. Here give this to the Missus, I expect she will need it to keep her strength up with the Blitz Kid and all.' He gave Dad the bar of chocolate.

The Blitz Kid, the Blitz Kid, yes that's his or her name.

CHAPTER 4

The Blitz Kid

It was getting on in the morning and I was feeling hungry, what had Dad prepared for us to eat I wondered. He read my thoughts for he sat down on a big stone and opened his bag. The thing about Dad was he always thought of everything and along with the things for Mum and the baby there was some food and water for us. We had just finished eating and were about to set off walking again when we heard a car approaching. It stopped without even a request. 'Hello you chaps,' a voice said, what me, a chap! 'I say would you like a lift.' The voice came from a young man in RAF blue. The car was very small, an open top with just two seats. 'We are going to Imtarfa hospital.' 'Come on jump in, 'said the man in blue. So we did and off we went at quite a rate of knots with me sitting on Dad's lap. 'I say old chap, do me a favour and fill my pipe will you, its in the glove compartment along with the tobacco and a light.' I thought Dad did rather well in filling the pipe, I remember

him saying something about watching his father
smoke a pipe. 'My name is George, by the way,
why are you going to the hospital.' By now Dad had
successfully given the pipe to our friend and lit
it so that he was puffing away whilst talking and
driving. I suppose you would call it driving of sorts,
if going flat out and dodging every bit of rubble at
full speed is driving then our hero can certainly
do it. Dad explained about Mum and how I came
to fetch him. 'I say,' said George, 'how exciting to
have a Kid born in the middle of the worst Blitz
since, well, since forever.'

Dad asked George what he did. 'I am a
Hurricane pilot, currently based at Takali right
next to the hospital. Things aren't going too well
at the moment. Hoards of them every day and
all day. Battle of Britain was nothing compared
to this. What makes it worse is no food, we are
down to one piece of bread given to us in the
cockpit waiting for fuel and ammo. At the end of
the day we search for anything to eat. At night
we Hurricane pilots together with a few Spitfires
pilots stand down. We have very little in the way of
night fighters just a few Beaufighters and a couple
of Wellingtons. It is rumoured that Spits are on the
way and about time to. They don't seem to realise
we will not give in, just give us the tools and we
will do the job.'

Dad just nodded in agreement, he always kept his thoughts to himself. It was obvious we were all suffering the same things. I could see on his face that his only concern right now was for Mum and the baby.

As we came close to the hospital we could see a raid was taking place. George slowed and said that as usual Jerry was supposed to be going for the 'drome and as usual they took aim over the big red cross at the front of the hospital. So it killed a few more innocents along with their own airmen who they knew were in the hospital, so what! They were told to eliminate Malta by the head of the Luftwaffe, Herr Goering and nothing was going to stop them.' Well we will see about that,' said George.

Dad told George to pull up at the bottom of the hill leading up to the hospital. George said he wished us well and hoped we will find Mum and the baby unharmed. Dad just nodded a thank you, he couldn't speak, he had that far away determined look on his face, just like when he thought Guiseppe was killed. George drove off in a cloud of dust heading for the airfield. No air raid was going to stop him.

Dad began to walk up the hill towards the hospital with me following. It looked fairly undamaged, there were quite a few more bomb

craters than when I left here almost two days
ago. Suddenly there was a woomf rather than an
explosion and I was thrown in the air. Dad was
knocked down and his tin hat went flying through
the air. Rubble came tumbling down the hill, just
missing us. Dad examined me for any injuries
and then himself. Nothing, except my ears were
ringing and I expect Dad's were as well. Dad was
running now and me with him. We could see a
large gaping hole in the side of the hospital. The
bomb blew half of the side away. There were beds
sticking out of what was left of the first floor. I
started barking that was where Mum was when
I last saw her. Dad could see what I meant and
started to climb up the rubble to the first floor.
By now Nurses and Doctors were emerging from
everywhere. Look Dad, I barked, here's Mum,
all covered in dust and alive. The Nurses quickly
wrapped Mum in sheets and they carried her
down until away from the hospital.

———————————

'Where is the child,' Dad asked Mum. 'The child,
your child, is a boy and he is somewhere in there,
he was very close to me before the bomb went
off.' Dad and I went off like dingbats. The bomb
came through the roof through the first floor
and exploded. Just a few feet from Mum and the

Blitz Kid. Luckily the blast went up because of the limestone. We panicked and started rushing around looking for the kid. I've found him, I've found him, I barked, he's here under this rubble, I stood over him. Dad rushed over and very gently moved the stones that covered him. He was breathing and looked okay, the clothing and sheets had protected him. 'Let's get out of here.'

We found our way down to ground level through all the rubble bits of bed and all the stuff you would expect to find in a hospital. Mum was there still wrapped up in sheets and lying on the floor.' So where is he,' she said. 'Don't worry, he is well and all in one piece,' 'Oh thank God I was so worried and yet I knew somehow that he was all right.' Mum is amazing, she was as calm as a cucumber. 'Give him to me, well what is going to happen now,' she was speaking to everybody, including Dad. Mum continued, 'You don't think I am going to lie here and wait for the next bomb to fall do you. I am moving and right now.' With that she gave Dad the Blitz Kid and stood up. Two nurses grabbed her and off we went around the other side of the hospital where there was very little damage. A place was found for Mum and the Blitz Kid along with the other survivors. I wasn't sure how many children were killed, Mum and Dad never spoke about it from that day forth. It

was decided that Mum and the Kid would stay in
the hospital for at least another week. Hopefully
that will give her enough time to get over the
shock of the bomb and the birth of the Kid. Dad
suddenly remembered the chocolate given to him
by the truck driver. It was a bit covered in dust but
the wrapper had saved it. Mum was very pleased
and she said it was even better than the present he
gave her on arrival from Gibraltar. That being of
course the bird.

Dad and I set off for Floriana, he knew the
chances of the hospital getting hit again were good,
on the other hand, he knew like Mum, they would
come through. 'He's a bonny wee Kid, isn't he?'
Smiled Dad. I barked in agreement. Yes the Blitz
Kid was indeed bonny. We were walking along
quietly, when our thoughts were interrupted by the
sound of a car, not any car but the car that took us
to near the hospital just the day before. 'Well I'm
blowed, so you made it then,' it was George, as he
screeched to a halt. ' I thought you had copped it
when that bomb went off. What about the missus
and the child?' 'They are fine and it is a boy.'
'Come on then jump in, I'm off to Valetta.' Dad was
inquisitive,' how come you aren't up there fighting.'
'It's like this, old boy, they bombed the hell out of
Takali, made holes everywhere. Probably the same
bunch as bombed the hospital. So the other boys at

Luqa and Hal Far 'dromes will do all the fighting
for a week. That means we have a weeks rest and
that means I am going to celebrate being alive and
now a double celebration for the Blitz Kid.' It would
seem that George drove everywhere at a vast rate
of knots, probably the same in his Hurricane. We
carried on like dingbats avoiding the large bits of
rubble going from one side of the road to the other
until at last we came to Floriana. 'This will do
nicely,' said Dad, 'I've no doubt we will meet again.
Perhaps you would like to meet the boy someday.'
'You mean the Blitz Kid,' shouted George, as he
roared off.

'Come on Stupid let's go home if it's still there
that is.' It was there just as we left it, the bombs
had fallen a few streets away. So Dad set about
organising the place for the Blitz Kid to sleep next
to Mum and Dad. Then we had to get hold of
Jessie, she was Maltese and going to help Mum
with the kid for the first few months at least. Mum
had arranged for Jessie to get all the clothes and
nappies ready for her return.

Meantime Dad went back on duty and I not
being able to look after Mum went with him. The
bombing never ceased, each day more and more
buildings were flattened. Dad said we had become
the most bombed place on earth. The only reason
people survived was because Malta is one big

rock of limestone, which can easily be tunnelled into. There are very few trees and very little wood in the houses, so the risk of fire was negligible. There is one thing above all else that will kill us all and that is starvation. The bombings on land were bad enough but the bombing and torpedoing of the ships trying to reach us were worse. Dad heard on the radio the Jerrys saying the Maltese were prisoners, all 250,000 of us. They hoped the Maltese would turn against the British. Well they are all like me, and they will never give in. We will win no matter what the odds are against us and at the moment they seem insurmountable. Dad looked at me and smiled, we both knew we will win.

Dad received a call from the CO, the hospital called, it was time for her and the Kid to come home tomorrow. We went home and told Jessie to get things ready. Dad sat down on the floor next to me and gave me a big cuddle. He said it was up to me to make sure that Mum and the Kid got back home safely. There would be an ambulance to bring her back and she would need me to be there with her.

I gulped down some food, had a drink and off I went. Only this time I will try and get a lift. Now then let me see I had to avoid civilian vehicles, not to be trusted, especially taxi cabs. Also to avoid army trucks, they might try and keep me. So that left cars like George's or ambulances. The chance of meeting George were very slim on the other hand somebody being injured and needing an ambulance going to Imtarfa were pretty good.

It wasn't long before I heard one approaching cautiously it was obviously carrying someone injured and it was doing its best to avoid large bits of rubble. There was only the driver in the cab, the other person must be inside attending to the injuries. I ran along the opposite side to the driver and jumped on the running board where he couldn't see me. It was great the bell would ring occasionally and all people, donkeys, military vehicles moved out the way. We soon pulled up outside the hospital where I jumped off. It looked a little different from the last time I saw it. Some of the bomb damage had been repaired.

I went searching for Mum, I found her sitting with the Blitz Kid waiting for the ambulance. When she saw me she let out a yell, I ran and jumped into her arms. She was so excited and happy to see me. 'Come and meet the Kid,' she said. I think she had forgotten we did meet briefly when I found him in the rubble. Any way she put me down beside him. I bent over him lying in his cot on the floor. Hello Kid, I am Stupid, your brother, I said in doggy language, barking that is.

He sort of gurgled. I am going to teach you how to talk to me.

It was getting dark and still no ambulance. Mum said we will have a problem because of the dark and the blackout. The ambulance with just the blackout lamps will take ages to get us home and there was every chance of a raid. Eventually it arrived, with just one driver and no assistant for Mum and the Kid. So off we set going at a snails pace with Mum, the Kid and me in the back. Once the door was shut it was pretty dark in there, with only a few slits of light coming through the sides. It was no surprise after half an hour to hear the air raid sirens. By the sound of the guns it looked like it was going to be a big one. The driver carried on for a while until a big one fell not too far away, close enough to rock the ambulance. It stopped and suddenly the rear door opened, the driver took one look inside, then he ran away.

Mum and I looked at each other, 'well,' she said, 'we cannot stay here and cool as a cucumber she picked up the Kid. Come on Stupid let's try and see where we are.' Once we were away from the ambulance I tried to remember where we were. It was no use everything seemed so different in the dark. We stood there wondering which way to go. There was a voice, 'excuse me missus,' said the voice, we looked but we couldn't see anyone.

I could smell someone, a man in army uniform. 'Look behind you,' said the voice, a man stepped down from an army truck. 'Did you just come from that ambulance.' 'Yes,' Mum replied. 'Where is the driver,' said the voice. 'I have no idea,' said Mum, 'he just ran away.' We could see the voice better now, he was an officer, with a very concerned face. 'He left you, this baby and the dog to fend for yourself in an unknown area, in the dark and in the middle of a raid. Come with me I will take you to the air raid shelter and you will describe the driver to me.' He led the way, we would never have found it in the dark. 'Now then, he said, describe him to me.' Mum did the best she could, it sounded about right to me, of course there was one thing missing, his smell. 'I'm going to leave you now, said the officer, and when the raid is over I will send two of my men to drive the ambulance and look after all of you until you get home.'

Mum looked at the Kid and me. 'We are going to be safe from now on.' The driver of the ambulance was never ever seen again.

The raid lasted the rest of the night, by dawn the all clear sounded and the two soldiers came to collect us. We reached home safe and sound and there was Jessie to greet us. What a fuss she made of the Blitz Kid. Smothering him with kisses and lots of cuddles. Mum soon got busy getting things just so. Dad came home and what a reunion we all had. Now we could settle into a real family life. True, we still had the problems of existing in trying to find food and then of course the bombing never ceased. Our lives were spent partly underground listening to the bombing and waiting for the all clear. Death was never far away. One day we had taken shelter and a Maltese family followed after us. The bomb fell a distance away, it was the blast that killed them. They didn't get into the shelter far enough for the blast to miss them. There was not a mark on them but they were dead, a mother and two children.

CHAPTER 5

Growing up

April continued with the food shortages steadily getting worse. Of course the bombing did not relent, day after day night after night, there was a continual noise that everybody had to endure. Dad said that a German General called Kesselring was determined to get Malta to surrender. He also said that a letter was sent to Kesselring about the deliberate bombing of Imtarfa hospital and it was mentioned that his own men were in the hospital as well as babies. There was no reply and they continued to use the hospital as an aiming point for Takali aerodrome.

It was the 15th of April 1942, when dad came home and said the civilians of Malta were given the George Cross by the King. This was the equivalent of the Victoria Cross for the military. The Governor made the presentation on behalf of the King. The medal says For Gallantry. The words that go with it say, bear witness to the heroism and devotion of its people.

'Does that mean I have it, the kid has it and of course Stupid must have it,' asked Mum. 'Well, yes I suppose so,' said Dad.

Mum was becoming very tired and altogether run down and I must admit I was feeling different, not going with Dad so much and lying around waiting for the next bite to eat. Then one day she broke, 'come on Stupid we are going to see Dad, I have had enough of this.' But, but, Mum I barked. 'Enough of your barking, we are going to see Dad and that is all there is to it.' Mum took hold of the Kid and off we marched.

Mum had that determined look on her face as we walked along a rubble strew path. A raid had only just finished, there was evidence of recently destroyed buildings. Some soldiers had just started to clear away the rubble and search for people who may be trapped. I could smell the awful smell of death. Mum stopped, 'I can hear water,' she said, and started to walk towards the sound. I jumped in front of her, barking and jumping to stop her. She mustn't go to where she thought the sound came from, it wasn't water, I could smell blood. Mum carried on walking. Soon we came to where Dad was working. There he was with Guiseppe repairing cables. He just looked at Mum there was no look of astonishment just resignation. 'I can't take anymore. I just can't.' She did not cry, she was well past crying. Her look said it all.

Dad was very quiet when he spoke to her. 'Look around you and you will see unexploded bombs. All have been defused and they are ready to be taken away for exploding. Until then another raid could set the load off.

You have put all of us in danger. So that we could all perish together. Up until now we stood a chance of this little family of ours surviving. Now I want you to go home and listen for every air raid warning. Go to the shelter and live underground until you hear the all clear.' When Dad gets very angry he goes quiet and he was very angry. Mum didn't say a word she just left and said, 'come on Stupid.' She never mentioned anything about it ever again.

Suddenly the air was full of new sounds, it was May and the promised Spitfires had arrived. The Blitz became worse, but this time we had the fighters to match Jerry. The odds were still in their favour, something like forty or fifty to one. It seemed impossible to get worse, but it did. At least this time we knew we were hitting back harder and the odds against were decreasing. Dad suggested we go in search of chocolate. The new pilots that had just arrived came in from an American carrier.

That meant they probably had some real chocolate with tin foil wrapped around it. I didn't matter to me, I still could smell chocolate a mile away.

Dad had an idea, instead of going to the harbour we would go to Valetta where he guessed the newly arrived pilots would be letting their hair down. We heard the noise a long time before we saw a number of them singing and making jokes. 'Well, well, look whose here, George.' George saw us and came over right away. 'I say how wonderful to see you, come on let's find a table and have a chat. So how's the wife and the Blitz kid.' Dad recalled the story. 'She broke down the other day, all I can say is she is putting up with remarkably well as is the kid. Tell me about yourself, I see the new Spitfires you were promised have arrived, I bet they have made a difference.' 'Not really, it was as if Jerry was waiting for them to arrive. No sooner had they landed the hoards came over and shot them to pieces. We lost 18 in the first few hours. I expect you've noticed a massive increase in the raids lately.' 'Well yes I have, Dad looked worried, 'but surely some must have survived.' 'The few that have are making a difference. I can give you an example, one 'drome, Luqa could only put up 4 Spits the other day and that was after scratching around for spares. We are shooting them down alright, 5, 6 or 7 to one. It is just that there are so many of them.'

Another pilot joined our table. 'This is Philip, he is a photo reconnaissance pilot.' Turning to Philip George said, 'I told you Phil, how I met these two on the way to Imtarfa hospital. They were going there for the birth of what turned to be a son.' Philip was most interested to hear about this and asked what day was the boy born. When he heard, this is what he said. 'I was returning from a recce job two days after your boy was born. At over 30,000 feet I had to wait until a raid had finished. I watched Jerry lining up for Takali and he purposely dropped his bombs on the hospital before going on to bomb the 'drome. It was a miracle your wife and the boy survived.' 'That's why we call him the Blitz Kid,' said George. 'It doesn't surprise me to hear what Jerry does,' continued George, 'they always try and kill our chaps who bail out. The other day I was in a fight with a 109 when a Spit crossed my path it was followed by two 109s they thought the pilot bailed out and they shot him to pieces. He didn't bail out, my 109 pilot did. It was him they shot to pieces. There was complete silence for a very long time. Let's look to the future, we are expecting another load of Spitfires shortly, only this time it will be handled differently. We now have quite a few spare pilots owing to the last mess up. So this time we will have them each allocated to a Spit and each Spit will have a full crew ready to re-fuel and re-load with ammo, ready for take off before Jerry has time to bomb and strafe.'

I can smell chocolate, loads of it, these airmen must have got plenty before they left that American aircraft carrier. It smells differently somehow, it must be the real chocolate Dad often talks about. I jumped down off of Dad's lap where I'd been listening to George and Philip talk. I ran to the nearest airman where I could smell chocolate, then back to Dad. 'I don't suppose any of you chaps can spare a bar of chocolate or two,' asked Dad. 'Well I don't have any,' said George, 'and I don't suppose Phil does either, Phil nodded in agreement. It wouldn't surprise me if a load of these blokes have some, having just come off an American aircraft carrier. I wouldn't mind betting they were showered by the Yanks with chocolate.' With that George called for silence and said. 'Now then you bods, we've got a Mum and a Blitz kid who need your help. It's a miracle they have survived so far, so let's help them to keep their strength up with chocolate. What about it, come on give what you can.' With that came bars of chocolate from everywhere. Dad was overwhelmed, I saw tears in his eyes for the first time in a very long time. He didn't know what to say. George could see how thankful Dad was and

51

put his arm on Dad's shoulder. 'Well cheerio for now, keep in touch, I want to see that lad grow up big and strong.'

Dad and I went home, this chocolate was going to last for ages. Mum was delighted she gave some to Jessie for all the help she was giving in looking after the Blitz kid. Dad hid the chocolate in what he said was a secret place. I didn't think it very secret I could smell it even outside the house. So I had better keep an eye on it in case any passing dog should come and investigate.

Mum said I was to stay with her and Jessie and look after the kid. I didn't mind as I was beginning to enjoy being with the kid. Just to watch him getting bigger every day and making baby noises was interesting. I decided to try and teach him my language after all if he can make noises like that why not doggy language. And so everyday I would bark the same bark until he copied it. The time passed quickly with each day being interrupted by the usual air raids, meaning we spent as much time underground as above it. Dad came home one day in late May and he said a great many Spitfires had arrived. He heard that this time the plan of having everything ready for their arrival had worked and Jerry had a major shock in getting a more even fight on their hands. So George was right, I hope he is okay.

July came and yet more Spitfires arrived. It
didn't stop the bombing though. The Blitz kid was
now 4 months old and learning fast, I could have
a reasonable conversation with him. Mind you, I
wish he would stop talking about food. Sometimes
I wonder if, well I just wonder that's all. August,
and Dad came home looking very dejected, he
said we only had a few days food left on the whole
island. He said the Governor was talking of jacking
it in. Of course he didn't actually hear him say
that, it was probably just rumour, but we certainly
were running out of food.

One day when we were all, that is Mum, the
kid, Jessie and me, were in the air raid shelter as
usual, we heard a bomb drop. This one was close,
very close. Although very deep, the whole shelter
shook, 'that was a close one,' said Mum. We waited
until the all clear sounded and then came out
to see masses of new rubble. There was a dust
cloud we couldn't see at first, then as it cleared we
climbed over the rubble to where our house was.
Our house didn't take a direct hit. It was enough
to destroy half of it. 'Well what are we going to
do now,' Jessie was terribly upset, it looked like
she was crying. The kid just looked into the sky, I
asked him what he was looking for. Those things
that make a noise, he said. I guess it is time for me
to teach some more doggy language.

Dad came home, he had seen the bomb drop.
It is strange, he seemed to know we would be
okay. It was Mum that was very angry. 'Well look
up there,' she said, 'how do you think I am going
to manage now.' We all looked to where she was
pointing. Her washing line that Jessie had just
strung up was high up where the roof once was.
On it was the Kid's clothes nappies and all. Mum
was distraught. 'We can't get any more, so what are
we going to about it and there's the chocolate, lost
forever.' Don't worry about a thing, I barked, Dad
and I will fix it. I was sure I could still smell the
chocolate but first of all the clothes and nappies.
Come on Dad I will show you the way through the
rubble and we can climb up through to next door's
roof which should give you a position to reach the
washing line. Dad followed me, we took our time
in carefully picking the way until we reached next
door's roof. Now it was up to Dad, he carefully
got to within reach of one end of the line still
attached to what was left of our roof. The other
end was flapping free and slowly he pulled in all
the washing. We retraced our steps and handed
the washing to Jessie. Now for the chocolate.
So much for Dad's secret place, I simply walked
over to where it was covered in rubble. It was the
American chocolate, Hershey bars all wrapped
in tin foil. Dad was delighted, 'now that will help

us all to keep strong.' Mum laughed and laughed,
'with you two around we will keep going forever.'
The house was repaired enough for us to carry on
living in it.

CHAPTER 6

Salvation

_____

It was the middle of August when Dad came home and said, 'Come on all of you, lets go to the harbour entrance, there are some ships that have got through.' Sure enough there are the ships including an oil tanker. This means we are saved. They look a bit battered to me, in fact on the deck of the oil tanker was the remains of a Jerry dive bomber. I hope they can unload before the next raid comes in. Jessie said it was the feast of Santa Marija and Dad called it operation Pedestal. Mum said she couldn't care less whatever it is called if it means we will get decent food at last, that is all that matters.

It didn't take long for Jerry to realise they would be in danger if they didn't destroy those ships. So they piled in constant air raids to try and destroy the ships before they could unload. Dad was on call day and night without a break. Jerry put the oil tanker on the floor of the harbour. It didn't catch light. Divers managed to connect pipes to the tanks and virtually all the oil was saved. The other ships carrying spare parts, ammunition and food were successfully unloaded.

For a few weeks we lived mostly underground. At least we had some decent food now. Mum and Jessie actually put on weight. Dad was going bald and Mum laughed saying it was because he had to wear his tin hat all the time. I taught the Kid doggy language, he was getting very good and I was enjoying myself more and more with someone to talk to.

September came and the Kid at six months was full of beans. We played for hours together and never stopped talking. It was noticeable by the end of September the air raids slackened off a little. Our Spitfires and night fighters were increasing in numbers. Then one day Dad said to me let's go with the Kid to Takali 'drome and see George. He would like to see the Kid. Is that okay Mum, for us to go and see George. Mum wasn't to happy at first but as the raids had virtually stopped she eventually agreed. Jessie packed some sandwiches, baby food, water and something for me. Just one bar of chocolate left, I'm afraid.

Off we set by bus this time, there must be enough fuel now for at least some sort of bus service. The bus was packed with Maltese. What a fuss they made of the Blitz kid, they all wanted to hold him and kiss him. Hold on there kid, I said to him, just grin and bear it. There was this dog on the bus and he could smell the chocolate. He came sniffing around hoping to get some. 'Just watch it chum,' said the kid, 'come any closer and Stupid here will sort you out.' Well you should have seen his face, totally shocked at hearing his own language, he turned away tail between his legs and never came near us for the rest of the journey.

We got off near the aerodrome and walked up to a guard who told us how to get to the pilot officers mess. It was now October and you should have seen the great numbers of aircraft all parked up in pens so that the chance of them being bombed was reduced. 'Hello George,' said Dad. A very surprised George said, 'welcome to our mess, I'm so glad to see you safe and sound. I must say I've been thinking about you and your little family. I was worried that the bombing had got you like so many others. So this is the Blitz kid, he doesn't look so bad in fact he looks very healthy to me.' 'Who is this joker,' said the kid, 'and has he got any chocolate.' George looked quizzically at the kid. 'What did he say, it sounded like a quiet bark.' 'Oh! He often talks like that,' said Dad, 'sometimes I think he is talking to Stupid.' I told the kid to be quiet or they could tumble us. Dad continued. 'It has been getting quiet down at the harbour, with

all the victories in North Africa, I think we have
turned the tide.' George agreed, 'We have certainly
seen the difference here. Look at all the aircraft
we now have and we are hitting Jerry were it hurts
most, in his supply lines. Malta is winning at last
and now with America beside us, dare I say it, we
cannot lose.'

Dad looked at his watch, 'It's time we were
getting back, this little lad needs his sleep. Before
we go'…. George interrupted him, 'I know you
want something more precious than gold dust.
Right, you chaps, listen up, this little lad has
come through the Blitz, in fact he is the Blitz kid
and he needs all the help you can give in the way
of chocolate. Dig into your pockets.' With that a
whole flurry of chocolate bars came and landed
on the table. George gave us one of those RAF
satchels and we stuffed it full. 'Thanks one and
all,' said Dad, 'and thank you George, we hope to
see you again.' When we arrived home and showed
Mum the chocolate, 'That should keep us going
until Christmas.'

Christmas, the kid will be almost nine months
old by then. I think now is the time for me to
teach him the finer parts of doggy language before
he learns human speak and perhaps a little more
in the way of getting around.

Dad came home one day and said that the air

raids would increase once again. Although we had a great victory in North Africa and the Americans were going to invade with us further along the coast in North Africa it would take some time before Jerry realised he was losing the war. That meant the ships were still not getting through in anything like the numbers we needed to stay alive. Mum was her usual self by saying. 'Well we have managed so far and we will just have to get on with it.' So it was the usual case of Dad going on duty and us going from our bomb damaged house to the air raid shelter.

CHAPTER 7

The end of the siege

November and Dad suddenly came home looking
ten years younger. He said we had finally pushed
back Jerry in North Africa and this time they
wouldn't recover. The Americans and the British
were going to push Jerry out of North Africa
altogether. This meant the siege was lifted and
food would soon be arriving. The kid didn't really
understand, all he kept on saying was does that
mean we will have some chocolate. Not really I
said, I bet it will take ages before we see any.

I've got an idea I said, you will be 9 months
before long and with a bit of help from me you
will soon be able to walk. Mum was watching us.
'What are you two up to, sometimes I'm almost
certain you are talking to each other. I hear the
kid muttering what sounds like soft barking noises
and I know Dad thinks the same. What about
you Jessie.' Jessie just smiled, I have noticed her
several times listening to us whilst she was doing
the washing. We will just have to be careful until

the kid speaks reasonably well in human language, then they will only hear what they want to hear.

Come on kid it's near Christmas and we need to be getting around and searching for chocolate. I thought that would get him going. So we begin, to start with you have to hold on to my collar. Then haul yourself up on two legs. Watch it you are wobbling, don't wobble and fall on me. 'It's alright for you with four legs,' said the kid.

Everyday when Mum and Jessie went out to hang the washing or go shopping, they would say now you look after the kid Stupid. Of course that gave us the opportunity to practice walking. Every day the kid got stronger until he could hold on to my collar and walk. Then he had to learn to run, we may need to run with what I had in mind. That took some time as his little legs needed the muscles but his determination won in the end. Now we were ready. So here's the plan kid, we go in search of chocolate which we will find in the pockets of the military. Now the siege has lifted there will be lots of new people who come on the Island with chocolate. We can play all sorts of tricks to get it. I will tell you where it is and you will get it. 'How can I get it out of their pockets,' Easy peazy, I said, first of all you simply ask for it, looking pathetic, a poor helpless boy who just needs chocolate to stay alive. 'Well that's quite

easy, because that's exactly what I am. What if
that doesn't work.' How about having a Mum, said
I, who is so thin she almost faints every day. 'That
also is true. So let's go and do it.'

The next day after Dad left to go on duty and
Mum went shopping with Jessie, the kid and I got
ready for our first outing. It was just a few days
before Christmas, ideal timing. The trouble was
being just nine months old his legs were still a bit
wobbly. I remember only too well trying to get up
steps when I was a pup and failing. That was when
Dad had found me. So instead of going down the
steps which lead to the harbour, we went along the
passageway being fairly level. It was still covered
with rubble which the kid could easily walk
around. Right oh kid grab my collar and stand up.
We had practised this so many times the kid found
it easy. Now we had to watch out for a returning
Mum and Jessie. Okay we'll just sneak along past
the shops to where there are a few troops still
clearing the rubble. I'll tell you when we find
someone with chocolate in their pockets. We
walked a little way, watching the soldiers at work.
Now here is a likely soldier, he has stopped work
for a cup of tea and yes he has chocolate in his top
pocket. 'Can I have some chocolate, mister,' the
kid blurted out. Oh no! not like that, I said. 'Go on
beat it,' boy was this one angry soldier, 'does your

Mother know where you are.' We turned and ran
back home. Luckily Mum and Jessie got there at
the same time. Mum looked at us for some time
before saying. 'Where have you two been.' Think
kid and think fast. 'Oh, Stupid and I were just
practising walking.' 'Well good,' Phew! And that
was all she said, although I did see a twinkle in
her eyes when she looked at Jessie.

Now look kid, let's practise this again, First we
walk a little further, then we find a spot, not too
quiet, just where a few military people are walking
by. This time we will try something different.
We sit down and I will rest my head on your legs
looking pathetic, you look the same. You know,
when Mum says you cannot have a thing, that
look. Then when Mr. or Mrs. come to that, there
are quite a few females in uniform as well now.
Anyway when the chocolate bar approaches I will
give you the nod. Then what, asks the kid. You will
mumble, oh, I'm so hungry, several times. Then
when they stop, you say, I don't suppose you have
any chocolate, very softly.

The next day Mum and Jessie are doing the
washing and then they will be going shopping,
they'll be gone for hours. Now is our chance come
on kid grab my collar and off we go. The men
who were moving the rubble have gone, thank
goodness. Let's go a few yards further on. There

are quite a few military people here and the chances are they have a ration of chocolate in their pockets.

We sit down, I rest my head on the kid's legs, looking cute in a pathetic sort of way. Ready kid here comes two a female and a male and she has the chocolate in her satchel. As they walk by the kid says, oh I'm so hungry. They carry on walking, I'm sure that kid said something, she said. She walked back, 'what did you say.' Very softly the kid said, 'Oh I'm so hungry, do you have any chocolate to spare.' At first she looked startled and sort of held her satchel closer. 'Well as a matter of fact I do, I suppose I could give you just a piece.' The kid pleaded again, 'Oh I'm so hungry and so is my Mum.' You could see it worked when she smiled, 'Go on then, here take it, the whole bar.' With that I stood up and wagged my tail in thanks.' Stupid and I are ever so grateful.' As soon as they were gone we ran home. When Mum and Jessie arrived there was a bar of chocolate on the table. Mum looked at it; we were in trouble. 'Right I want an explanation. How did you get the chocolate bar.' We were out practising walking,' said the kid, 'and this lady gave it to us.' I barked in agreement. 'Wait until your Dad gets home, we will see what he has to say.'

Dad came home and looked at the chocolate and listened to what Mum had to say. Then he looked at us, 'well I don't think they could have stolen it, nobody would have left any chocolate where it could be stolen. After all it's rarer than gold dust. So it must be true and just in time for Christmas, we will all have a share.'

For the next few days we had a reasonably quiet Christmas. Not much food but at least we had some chocolate. I suspect Mum wasn't to sure about the kid and me, she never said anything, it was just the way she looked at both of us. Anyway, Dad had a few days off and he said it would be a good idea if the kid and Stupid went and had a look at what was left of the harbour. Mum thought it a good idea as well, but instead of Dad carrying the kid why not see if he can walk especially by hanging on to Stupid's collar. Oh Oh! This could be trouble, I said to the kid. Mum suspects something is going on. We'll just have to be canny about this. 'What do you mean,' All you need do, I said, is say carry me Dad, every now again, especially going up steps. I can't go up steps anyway.' Okay, ask Dad to teach you then, I said, that will save us a lot of time later. Mum was watching us carefully. 'There you are I told you, those two can talk to each other,' Dad just thought it was nonsense. Although he remembered George noticing something as well.

'Come on you two, let's go.' Dad was keen to get

walking. Over the next few days we went walking right into the new year. Each day we would go up and down steps and each day the kid became stronger.

CHAPTER 8

1943

Dad came home one day and told us about the Royer family. They are going to be evacuated, Mum asked where to. South Africa, and Dad had requested if we can be on that ship as well. He was told by the CO that as we have been on the front line since this war began and really suffered through the Blitz, meaning all of us, we will get priority for a place on board the ship. Does that mean I can come as well, I said barking. Yes of course you will come, you are part of the family.

Days past and there was no news about us being evacuated.

Dad was early, he just stood there looking at Mum. 'What on earth is wrong with you.' 'The ship is in for the evacuation,' said Dad, 'but I am not on it.' 'Does that mean I could be on it.' 'Yes, you the kid and Stupid.' Jessie cried. Mum was very angry, 'well you can tell the army, they have broken their promise and I am not leaving without you. You can remind them that you did your 21 years service

before this war started and you have fulfilled your
obligation to this empire. We should be in New
York by now with your brothers.' Dad spoke very
quietly, 'I know, the CO and I knew you would
say that. He has done everything to reverse the
decision, they will not. I am wanted for something
special, somewhere I can't tell you about.' There
was a long pause, 'in that case, you can tell the
CO I will most definitely be staying here with you.'
The Royer family with many others left Malta,
Mum didn't go to see the ship leave. At least Jessie
was happy.

Things got back to normal for us. Food was
still short and we still lived in the bombed out
house. Dad worked on the clearing up process,
repairing cables and getting things working again.
Mum went shopping with Jessie plus all the usual
household chores. There was one important thing
missing, chocolate. It was time the Blitz kid and
I got into action. He was much stronger now with
Dad making him go up and down all those steps to
the harbour.

Right come on kid, Mum and Jessie are out for
a few hours let's go. Only this time we go where
there are lots of new military coming to Malta. I
know why, said the kid, it's because we won big
victories and now we are preparing for an invasion
somewhere. That means the Americans are here,

I said, and that means Hershey bars. Hershey, Hershey what's that, said the kid. That means real chocolate wrapped in tin foil, I said. Come on grab hold of my collar. What a difference a couple of months make. This time the kid and I flew down the steps towards the harbour.

We soon reached a likely spot where all sorts of military were going by in trucks and walking. Now this time we'll play it differently, I said, I will walk a few paces in front of you and when I smell chocolate I'll tell you. You immediately fall down. Stay down until he or she helps you to stand. I bet the person then says are you alright and you say, not really, looking a bit wobbly. Then what do I do, said the kid. Look you'll soon get the hang of it, I said. Not really knowing what will happen.

Here comes a likely American soldier, I started walking a few paces in front. He's got chocolate in the top pocket of his tunic, I said. The kid fell down. 'What the heck,' said the soldier, 'Here kid let me help you up. Poor kid he looks half starved. What can I do to help you,' 'I don't suppose you have any spare chocolate,' 'Why I sure do, here you are, just a minute,' he turned and shouted to his buddies, 'hey you guys, can you spare a few chocolate bars for this poor half starved kid.' Hershey bars, three of them, came flying through the air at the kid. 'Cor, thanks mister, that will keep the family going for ages.' 'Your welcome kid,' was the reply. The kid put the four bars in his pockets and we went home.

'I just don't believe it'. This time Mum was really upset. 'When Dad gets home he will have to sort it out'. I suppose Dad was getting fed up with us turning up with chocolate, so he took us to one side and gave us the third degree. 'Tell me exactly how you got the chocolate.' The kid did tell exactly how. He fell down right in front of this American soldier who helped him get up. And then he gave us the chocolate. I wagged my tale and barked, it's the truth. Dad looked puzzled, 'why weren't you holding on to Stupid's collar and why did the soldier just give you the chocolate. On the one hand it sounds not quite right, but on the other hand it does. The Americans are always very generous. So we'll leave it like that.' Dad told Mum the story and they will just have to believe the kid until they know differently. In the meantime he suggested we all enjoy the chocolate.

It was June 1943 and we were expecting a visit from somebody called the King. He was coming by ship and then going around the Island seeing people. Dad was on duty as usual and Mum didn't feel like celebrating after the shock about the evacuation. I would like to see him and the kid said he would as well. Jessie said she would take

71

us, so off we went. There were crowds everywhere climbing on the rubble, lining the streets, climbing lampposts, trying to find a vantage point. The kid and I soon lost Jessie. No good for chocolate here kid too many civilians and far too crowded. Look out, he's coming, let's crawl between the legs of these people and have a look. We crawled to the front of the crowd and there he was, very smart in his officer's uniform and shaking hands with people. I noticed the kid was going to speak but before I could stop him he uttered the words. 'I don't suppose you have any chocolate'. The king looked down and I heard him mutter what did he say. One of the officers accompanying the king said something to an RAF officer keeping back the crowds. The officer turned and looked at us. Oh Oh! It was George. Quick let's go and we turned to run. 'Just a minute,' it was George who came into action, 'I know you two don't I, it's Stupid and the Blitz Kid, isn't it. Now then did I hear correctly was there something about chocolate being asked for or what?' Admit to nothing kid, keep quite. 'Now the king has passed,' it was George again, I think I will take you two home.' With that he lifted both of us under each arm and we headed for home. 'Tell me how to get there,' he said to the Kid. 'Do you think I should'. It was the kid talking to me, yes of course I said. 'Suppose he

tells Mum about me asking for chocolate'. Well
we will just have to say that is what we thought
Kings were for, asking for things that is. George
suddenly stopped and put us down. We sat down
on some rubble. George stood there looking at us
for at least a minute, 'At first I wasn't sure, now I
am sure, you two can talk can't you?' Go on tell
him kid, I think we can trust him. 'Yes' said the
kid. George took off his cap, laid it beside him,
then took his pipe and tobacco out of his tunic and
carefully filled and lit it. Clouds of smoke issued
forth through which he spoke. 'Now what should
I tell your Mum, I don't suppose she knows about
the chatting you two are doing does she, or about
the chocolate hunting. Oh and by the way, I have a
bar of Hershey's best here. We'll split it three ways
and have it now. As I was saying I don't want to
give the game away, after all nobody is getting hurt
and all that is happening is the chocolate being
used for better purposes. So the story is I saw you
watching the King and because of the crowds, I
thought it better to escort you home. Which in
any case is quiet handy because I wanted to meet
your Mum and see your Dad.' I wagged my tail
and barked a lot in thanks. 'Right let's go.' George
continued but only after finishing his pipe.

Jessie had returned without us, Mum was not
worried, she knew we would be okay. She was just

beginning to get angry for being late when she saw us coming with a RAF officer.

'Hello, how do you do', said George, 'you must be Mum, I'm George.' Mum's anger disappeared quickly when she remembered Dad talking about George. 'Would you like to come in for a cup of tea.' George said yes and the two sat talking for ages about the war. George wondered why we were not evacuated when the siege was lifted. Mum explained about Dad's service record and the army refusing to let him go and she wouldn't go without him. I heard Dad coming home and the kid and I went to meet him. The kid told him that George had brought us home and he was talking to mum. Dad was pleased to see George still in one piece. 'Well George now you have met the whole family and how are you?' 'I'm well thanks. It was fortunate I met your two ragamuffins watching the King because I needed to see you all. You see, George continued, my time is up in Malta and I have orders to return to GB at the end of the month.' No more chocolate from there then, the kid whispered to me in doggy. George looked at us guessing what was said. Dad said he would miss him and Mum thanked him very much for the chocolate as it certainly helped the family to pull through difficult times. With that it was just a simple Cheerio to everybody and George was gone.

CHAPTER 9

Where is Dad

It was late July when Dad walked in one day and started to pack his kit bag. Mum looked at him for some time, it was obvious that Dad was finding it hard not to break down in front of us.

Mum waited until Dad stopped to look for something, 'well what is going on.' She said. Dad explained that he had received orders to embark on a troopship in the harbour. He wasn't allowed to tell anyone where he was going only that to be onboard by a certain time. We all looked at each other not wanting to believe what we are hearing. Mum said, 'What will become of us.' Dad made us sit down in front of him and he told us that he knew we would be okay. He told the kid and me that we are to look after Mum. Mum tried not to cry and she turned away so as not to let Dad see how upset she was. He hugged us all and kissed Mum goodbye. It wasn't cheerio it was goodbye and he was gone. We didn't know where, just gone.

The next day the kid and I went out and walked round the harbour. There were no ships. So he really was gone. When we got back Mum was talking to Jessie. She was saying goodbye. Jessie bent down and gave us a cuddle it was goodbye time for her as well. So what about us, Mum the kid and me, where were we going? Mum soon made it clear we were going to a place called Sliema. Married quarters, she said.

Sliema 1943 – Married Quarters

Married quarters turned out to be a home with other families like us in similar homes. It was comfortable but of course there was something missing; no Dad. Mum got on with the neighbours all right, except when we alone, she went very quite and kept on saying, 'What will become of us.' I told the kid to say, don't worry Mum we'll be all right.

There was much to explore in our new surroundings. For a start we were slap bang next to the American army, navy and air force head quarters. As you can imagine the kid and I thought this marvellous. Mum on the other hand didn't. She wasn't getting any sleep and for that matter I was finding it hard as well. The kid slept like a log.

Well one day Mum blew up and marched to see the American CO. Oh no, we thought, this is going to ruin our chances of getting chocolate. She

76

charged into the CO's office and gave him what for. Much to our surprise Mum came back full of smiles, saying they promised to keep the noise down from now on. Surprise, she was given two chocolate bars for us. They kept their promise and Mum and I always slept well after that.

One day the kid and I were out scouting when we came across a parade ground full of soldiers. There was a man stood on a Jeep in the middle with all the soldiers around him. The kid was more than interested in the man in the middle, 'I wonder if?' Oh no you don't I said, you messed up last time with the King. Let me go and see what's going on, you stay here. I went between the legs and right to the front where the man was talking. Sniffed, and immediately returned to the kid. No joy kid, all he smells of is cigarettes, lets go home. We turned and started walking back when we heard several Jeeps approaching. They stopped beside us, we ignored them. A voice said, 'Hey you kids do you want a lift?' we looked, it was the man who was in middle of the parade ground. Before I could stop him the kid said, 'No thanks mister, you smell of cigarettes and we want chocolate.' Everybody in the Jeep and all the other Jeeps burst out laughing including the man who spoke to us. 'Well now let me see, any of you guys got any chocolate.' 'We sure have General.' They said. The

General spoke again, 'come on kids get in, my guys will give you some chocolate. Now where exactly are you going?' The kid explained we live right next door to his HQ. The General dropped us off outside our house and it was fortunate that Mum was watching. No questioning about how we got the chocolate then. She simply said, 'So now you know General Eisenhower as well,' and she smiled.

Mum told us the General was in Malta for the invasion of Sicily. The kid and I wondered if Dad was going to invade Sicily. He asked her, 'Mum do you think that is where Dad has gone, somewhere for the invasion of Sicily?' I don't think so she said because he would have stayed here if that were the case. I just have no idea where he is. What will become of us.' Every time Mum said, 'what will become of us,' which was often. We replied, don't worry Mum we'll be all right. At least the kid said that, I just wagged my tail and barked.

It became the good time for us, well as good as it could get without Dad. Being next to the American HQ there was always good quality food being sent over from the kitchens. The kid and I were given lifts on the Jeeps all over the Island. We became quite famous, there goes the Blitz kid and Stupid people shouted as we went by. The soldiers loved it as well. I noticed every time we stopped there were always quite a few ladies

hanging about and it wasn't just to give us a cuddle
or for the chocolate.

One day as we were driving along I spotted a
British soldier, or rather I smelled a soldier that
I recognised. Stop the Jeep kid, quick. The kid
asked the driver to stop and we piled out. Just wait
here and do as I say. Look at this soldier coming
towards us, well I know him. He never became
thin in the siege. I reckon he was hoarding stuff
especially chocolate. Dad and I tricked him last
time we met and we are going to do it again. No
doubt he will recognise me, so everything will have
to be quick. I will run towards him and bite him
on the ankle. Whilst he is hopping about you will
give him a hefty kick on the other leg. He will hit
the ground and I will tell you where the chocolate
is. It all went like clockwork, the chocolate is in
the top pocket, the kid grabbed it. 'I know who you
are,' said the soldier trying to get up, 'I'll get the
police on to you.' 'Oh yeah, and we know what you
have been doing fatty, just you try.' We beat it and
waited for a Jeep to go by. It didn't take long, 'You
two look pretty happy with yourselves.' Said the
driver. We did, we sure did.

The months went by, there was no news from
Dad. Mum wasn't too worried about that, he was
probably working on secret work and in any case
she would have needed to get someone to read

the letter. It was just every now and again, when nobody was within ear shot, she would say, 'What will become of us,' We always answered, don't worry Mum we will be all right.

November 1943

There was a great deal of excitement around the whole array of army buildings and married quarters. Mum said a man who was very important, like the General, was going to visit us, his name was Churchill. The day came and all the soldiers, American, British, Canadian, Australian, New Zealand, South African, Indian and many others lined up to see him. We could see everything from the married quarters with the parade ground right in front of us. When he finished walking the lines of troops he gathered all of them around him for a talk. 'Go on then,' it was the kid talking, 'go and see if he's got any.' Off I go running between the legs until I reach the front. He was just finishing his talk and lighting a cigar. No chance of chocolate here then and I turned to go back. Then I heard him say, 'I want to see a child, a survivor of the blitz.' An officer accompanying him said he would clear the parade ground first. I raced back to Mum and the kid. No chance there kid he always seems to have a cigar on the go. Mum heard us, 'you two at it again.' I looked at the parade ground it was empty except for two figures, Churchill and the officer, they were coming this way.

'Good morning Madam, I am Winston Churchill.' 'Yes I know who you are,' said Mum. 'and this is your child,' he continued, 'the Blitz kid and his companion, Stupid. Famous throughout the Island for getting extra chocolate rations. Now what can I do for you?'. Up piped the kid, 'well we certainly don't want a cigar, I think you know what we want.' Churchill laughed and said, 'nice little chap,' and patted him on the head, 'see to it, the chocolate that is.' The officer made a note of it. They walked away. So now we know Churchill as well as the King and General Eisenhower.

The chocolate came as promised and Mum decided to put some aside for Christmas. Although we were receiving food and some very good food from the American kitchens there was always the thought it wouldn't last. The Blitz kid and I were having a rare old time going around the Island in Jeeps with our American friends. I guess you could call it a two way thing, we loved to ride everywhere and our friends loved all the attention they would get when we were with them, especially from the girls.

It was on one of these occasions that I thought

I spotted my first Mum. I told the kid to ask for
the Jeep to stop and out we jumped. Come on run,
I saw her going down a passageway. Yes it is her
all right, Mum, I shouted, she turned and what
a reunion we had. This is the Blitz kid, I said.
Well I've heard a lot about you, it's all over the
Island. 'Pleased to meet you.' Said the kid. Mum
was stunned, you can speak doggy? 'Of course,
I have the best teacher in the world.' Mum got
her voice back, well you are not so Stupid now,
I always knew you were the clever one. I had to
ask, so what happened to the rest of the family?
She thought for a while, oh! they are fine just fine.
I wondered why she had to think about it before
replying. I didn't push it any further. Well Mum
my other Mum will be wondering where we are.
My Mum looked old and frail, I just didn't know
what to say. It's all right son, she said, we all get
old, and this war took a lot out of me. The time
has come to say goodbye. It was nice to meet you
kid. Goodbye Stupid.

    I stood there and watched her walk away,
goodbye Mum and thanks for everything, I love
you. We caught a Jeep home.

December 1943

There was something big going on all the military
were smarting things up. The soldiers took us to
Luqa airfield and we watched them preparing for
the visit of someone important. A Jeep was made
ready, it had a special seat for this person. Go on
ask that airman over there who is coming I said
to the kid. 'Excuse me mister,' for one moment I
thought he was going to ask for chocolate, 'excuse
me mister, why does that Jeep have a special seat,
who is it for?' You could see the airman wasn't sure
about giving an answer, eventually he said, 'now
keep it dark kid, it's for the President of the United
States.' The kid replied, 'don't worry mister I won't
tell anybody.' Little did the airman know that he
already told me.

We walked away and the kid asked, 'who
is this guy,' it's the bloke who sends us all the
chocolate. 'Wow is it really him, he must be very
rich, everybody says the chocolate is worth more
than gold dust.' Yes I guess so. 'Cor if we can get
a lift here when he arrives we may be able to have
chocolate to last until the end of the war.' When we
arrived home Mum was looking depressed, 'what
will become of us.' We said together, 'don't worry
Mum we'll be all right'. 'Here just a minute,' it was
Mum, 'you both said that together in doggy. I knew
it I just knew it.' We all laughed and laughed.

83

A Jeep pulled up in front of the house. 'Come on kid and Stupid, jump in. This is it, the day the big boss arrives.' The jeep was really packed, we managed to squeeze in, and off we went. The airfield was full of military, navy, air force and army from British and American forces. They all lined up ready for inspection. An aircraft had already arrived bringing the President and the Jeep with the special seat was waiting at the bottom of the steps of the aircraft.

'He looks a bit wobbly,' said the kid, 'I can see why a special seat was made for him in the Jeep.' I heard one of his men saying he has something called polio. This makes it hard for him to walk, anyway look he is in the Jeep and beginning the inspection. 'We won't be able to get near him, going up and down the lines in the Jeep.' I expect he will stop sometime, I said. He did and then all the men and women from all the nations on parade gathered round him. 'Now is our chance, let's go.' We picked our way through every body until we got to the front. Boy, he was high up in the special seat and he was making a speech to everybody about Malta. He just finished when a voice said, 'thanks for all the chocolate mister President,' guess who said it. The President looked puzzled. 'What did he say?' 'I said thanks for all the chocolate, that's what I said and I meant it.' The whole parade ground burst out laughing including the President. 'Well that's all right kid, you're welcome.'

Everybody was happy and laughing, we were carried off the parade ground given loads of chocolate and taken home. Mum heard what happened and said, 'so now you know the President of the United States as well.'

It was Christmas once again and the food was adequate except we had plenty of chocolate to go around. There were now other children to play with, all belonging to service families. They of course shared in our good fortune with the chocolate. The Military were far less in numbers now. Mum said some were going to Italy and others to England in preparation for the invasion. There was talk of us leaving Malta but we didn't know where or when.

CHAPTER 10

1944

We were told to get ready to leave there would be a ship arriving shortly to take us somewhere. Mum went to see the officer in charge to find out more. She came back disappointed. 'He didn't know where or when. What will become of us.' 'Don't worry Mum, we'll be all right,' we said. There was laughter all round.

The ship did not arrive. Nor the next one. Nor the next one. 'I'm sick of all these promises, it's just like the army when we were promised to go to South Africa, they broke that promise. There's one good thing I suppose when the ship eventually turns up it will be easy to pack up ready to go. We have nothing except the clothes we stand in plus a few sheets and tablecloths.' The kid and I looked at each other, we didn't know what other things people had. It seemed to us we had everything we needed.

Winter turned to Spring, The kid and I were
kicking around a bit. The military were far less
in numbers and so was the chocolate. It was a
boring time, we played with the service children
and waited. One day the word came of another
ship coming for us. 'I'll wait until I see it before I
believe it.' Mum was completely fed up with the
promises. The kid and I walked to the harbour
and sat on the wall watching for a likely looking
ship. 'Hey what's that over there?' It was the kid,
I don't know it looks like a cargo ship to me. 'Let's
go down and find out.' Okay I said, we ran down
to where they were unloading some stuff from
the ship. 'I'll ask this sailor what's going to happen
when the ship is empty.' Don't ask for chocolate,
this bloke looks like he'll give us a thick ear rather
than any chocolate, anyway he stinks of rum or
something. 'Mister, excuse me, what are you doing
with this ship once unloaded?' 'None of your
business,' said the sailor. I told you so, try another
idea, ask him if he is looking forward to going to
Blighty. So the kid did. 'Blighty, Blighty you bet
your life I am and the sooner the better.'

We ran back to Mum and told her a ship was in
and it was returning to England. She immediately
went to the officer told him of the ship. It was
some time before we heard from him and yes that
is the ship we will be on. Was it going to England

she asked. Yes, she was told the destination is Liverpool. Mum was ever so pleased, perhaps we will be heading nearer to Dad.

We packed everything into one suitcase and we were ready.

CHAPTER 11

April 1944 – Where is Home

There weren't many goodbyes to say, most of the families came onboard with us. It was to Jessie where Mum had the hardest time in saying goodbye. They both cried knowing they would never see each other again.

The dockside was crowded with children and their mothers milling about everywhere. A surprising number of women were Maltese who had married army, navy and air force personnel. We all lined up to board the ship which wasn't designed to carry passengers. An officer showed us to our bunks, which was wooden slats, one above the other. He looked at me, 'that is not allowed.' Mum wasn't happy, 'his name is Stupid and he is my son's companion, they are inseparable. If it wasn't for him my son would have died. Stupid is my other son and he stays with me or we will get off now.' 'Shall I kick him in the ankles.' Said the kid. 'What did he say, it sounded half a bark and half words.' The officer looked puzzled. He could see Mum meant it. 'I'll go and see the Captain,' and with that he left.

We looked around it was dark, no light except for one light bulb. 'Surely we don't have to spend however long it takes to get home here.' 'Mum, where is home,' yes where is home I barked very softly. 'Well you were both born in the army and you kid were registered in London. The home you both have is the army. Wherever you decide your home is, that is where it is.'

The officer came back, 'the Captain wants to see all of you now.' We all followed him to a nice cabin with several chairs scattered around. The Captain was sitting behind a desk twiddling with a pen and looking at a sheet of paper. 'Please sit down, there's nothing on here about a dog called Stupid, just a family of three.' 'Well that's what we are ,' Mum was still upset from her talk to the officer, 'we are that family of three and nothing will separate us.' There was a pipe on the desk, the Captain picked it up, took out a tobacco pouch from his pocket and carefully loaded his pipe. 'I suppose,' he said lighting the pipe and issuing great clouds of smoke, 'I suppose this war has created all sorts of anomalies that break the rules and perhaps I should create another one. I have heard of these two,' he said looking at the kid and Stupid, 'in a bar last night. They have become quite famous in their hunt for chocolate. No bad reports mind, so I think I'll use the Nelson touch and turn a blind eye to Stupid. Carry on family of three.'

'He was a nice man,' said Mum. 'Do you think,' before the kid could get any further, Mum said, 'certainly not, he has been good to us and I don't want you bothering him for any chocolate. In any case this ship just came from England and the chances of finding chocolate here aren't very good.' We returned to our bunks feeling good on the one hand, as we were staying together and bad on the other. Here we are going to live in almost blackness and no chocolate to cheer us up.

The ship started up and we began to pull out of Malta. Up on deck the sun was shining, there were a few people waving goodbye, we waved, although there was nobody we knew. Mum became upset, I guess the memories hit her pretty hard. As always at times such as this she said what will become of us and as usual we replied don't worry Mum we'll be all right, ending up with all of us laughing.

The kid and I stayed on deck when Mum went below, to straighten things out. Ships formed up it great lines, destroyers, cruisers, an aircraft carrier and a battleship. Mum said one of the kid's uncles is on a battleship, the Resolution I think, I wonder if he is watching us right now. The kid asked one of the sailors, 'what are the ships doing.' 'They

91

are forming a convoy, with all ships like us in the middle and all the Royal Navy ships protecting us on the outside.' I looked at the kid, ask him what does he mean protecting. 'It's in case of U-Boats, German undersea boats with torpedoes. There aren't too many aircraft around any more, thank goodness. Come on now you two cannot stay here on deck go down to your Mother.'

So it's them again still trying to kill us even now at sea. The ship was moving, we could hear the engines and feel it going up and down. The kid said his tummy felt funny and Mum told him not to worry he would get used to it. It was dark with just the one light bulb burning all the time. We could hear voices all around us, but we couldn't see any people just shadows. The mealtimes were served in shifts, the food was good. During daylight hours we were allowed to go on deck and watch the Destroyers racing up and down the length of the convoy. Protecting us as the sailor said. So this is how the sailors lived, nothing much seemed to be happening most of the time. At least being on a Destroyer something was happening all the time.

After a day or two of walking up and down the same stretch of deck the kid and I were getting bored. On Malta it was a case being on the go all the time. Getting lifts from the military to and from the airfields, watching the aircraft going on missions to Italy, by the end of each day we were exhausted. It was always great fun being made a fuss of and perhaps getting some chocolate. Here it was day three and we were totally fed up.

Suddenly a commotion started by a few Maltese women who pointed out to sea. A U-Boat! U-Boat! They shouted. 'Mr. Trimble, get down there at once, tell those women to shut up immediately, and explain to them why there is no U-Boat,' it was the Captain speaking. Mr. Trimble came at the double, he soon had the situation under control and quietly explained why there is no U-Boat. He then ordered them below deck and was about to do the same to us when came a shout from above. 'You two, this is the Captain speaking, yes you two,' it was the Captain and he meant us, 'come up here right now.' We climbed to the bridge where the Captain was pacing up and down, he was muttering to himself, something about silly women. 'I have been watching you for three days now and you look bored stiff. I can guess why after all the excitement you were getting in Malta. Well I might have a job for you both and if you carry it out well you never know, there could be a chocolate bar or two for payment.' We looked at each other in disbelief. 'What do you say to that?' We both nodded yes. The Captain was muttering again, 'I could have sworn Stupid understood everything I said.' He continued, 'Right you are then, let me explain. The convoy is zigzagging down the Mediterranean sea, incidentally do you know what zigzagging means, no.' He showed us by moving his hands to one side then the other. 'We are doing this to confuse U-boats, E-boats and planes. There aren't many enemy left in this sea now but a juicy convoy such as this may tempt them to try. What is needed is as many eyes as possible looking at the sea and air. My guess is in Malta you saw many enemy planes and therefore you can spot one a mile away, is that correct?' We both nodded again. He gave me a strange look when I nodded. 'Now all I have to do is tell you how to spot a U-boat. You won't see an E-boat because they only operate at night and the Navy have strong searchlights for them. U-boats are a different matter and this is what you have to look for.' He took his pipe out of his pocket and held it upright. He then moved it through the air and with the other hand he pretended that was the sea so the pipe stood above the sea. 'All you will see is the pipe, I mean periscope sticking up and a wake behind it, understood?' We both nodded again. This time he shook his head and muttered, 'I must be going crazy. Too long at sea that's the problem.' He needed a pipe, which he carefully

94

loaded and lit. Great clouds of lovely smelling
smoke filled the bridge. 'Now then remember we
have an aircraft carrier somewhere out in front
and destroyers searching for the enemy, so don't
get it wrong with our aircraft.' Tell the Captain we
know the difference in more than one way with
the aircraft. I was barking very softly. The Captain
was watching very closely. 'Don't worry Captain we
know the difference between our aircraft and the
enemy not just by looks they all make a different
sound as well.' The Captain nearly bit through his
pipe, he mumbled something about getting leave
after this trip. He looked way into the distance,
puffing on his pipe. 'What if,' he thought for a bit
and had a couple of puffs, 'what if you two come
on the Bridge first thing after breakfast each
day to begin your spotting. Once you hear or see
something tell the officer of the watch, which
is Mr. Trimble or me. Is that clear?' Yes sir, we
both said together. I heard the Captain talking to
himself as we went back to Mum it sounded like,
I must be nuts. Mum was really pleased we had a
job to do that would keep us out of mischief.

The first day on the Bridge we looked at the
sea then we looked at the sky, nothing. If it carry's
on like this it's as boring as on the deck. When it
came to lunch times, we had to say, permission for
lunch sir and the reply was always the same, carry

on kid and Stupid. It was the fifth or sixth day,
I don't remember which when we heard a plane.
What do you reckon asked the kid, definitely yes I
replied. 'Captain we can hear a plane approaching
and now we can see it.' 'What, impossible,' he said,
'radar must have picked it up.' 'Well there it is just
skimming above the water.' 'Mr. Trimble tell the
radio operator enemy aircraft bearing 3 o'clock.
Let's get those Destroyers into action.' There was a
splash, 'oh no, it's a torpedo, hard a starboard.' We
all watched the torpedo go past our bow. 'That was
a close one, now how did that happen?' It was the
Captain talking to Mr. Trimble. 'I've no idea sir, it
must have been so low it didn't show on the radar.'
'Well go and find out, if it wasn't for our pair of two
special eyes and ears we would have been blown to
bits and find out what happened to that plane.' 'Aye
aye sir,' and with that Mr. Trimble disappeared
at the double. 'Well now you two that calls for a
celebration. How about breaking out a couple of
Hershey bars.'

We went down to see Mum feeling mighty
pleased with ourselves. That night we slept like
logs with lovely chocolate in our tummies.

I began to lose all sense of time and I know the
kid did, he kept on saying to Mum are we nearly
there yet. She replied, 'I haven't the foggiest idea,
why don't you ask the Captain.' Okay, so we did,

'Captain where are we and are we nearly there yet?' The Captain looked at the kid, 'I thought you might like to know how we were nearly blown to bits by that plane first.' Yes please, we both nodded together, the Captain smiled, I think he had got to know our secret by now. He loaded his pipe and between puffs he told us what happened. 'Well it didn't come from Italy and it didn't come from Africa, both places are in Allied hands now. It could only come from one place, Corsica. That is a French island and it must have been a last ditch effort on their part because the allies will soon have it under control. Unfortunately it was too low for the Destroyers guns and it got away. Anyway well done you two.' The smell of his pipe was gorgeous, we loved it. 'So where are we now?' 'Come over here and look at this chart. All this zigging and zagging has taken us twice as long to get out of the Mediterranean. We shall be approaching Gibraltar tomorrow night. I know your Mum comes from there so you had better give her the bad news, she wont be able to see it in day light then the good news, there is no blackout in Gibraltar so she will see all the lights. After we've come through the Straits of Gibraltar we head down the coast of Africa. It's the long way round to Blighty. There is no choice because U-boats still operate out of French ports and we are still going

to zigzag.' The kid and I looked at each other we
didn't really understand except it was going to take
a long time, a really long time. We finished our
duty on the bridge and went below.

We knew that Mum was looking forward to
seeing Gibraltar, after all she hadn't seen it for
years and it was her home. Leave it to me, said
the kid, 'Mum, tomorrow night we will go passed
Gibraltar which is good news because there is
no blackout on Gibraltar you will see it all lit up.'
Mum didn't say a word she turned away so we
couldn't see. She was crying. The next day on the
bridge was uneventful. We went to bed as usual,
Mum didn't sleep she went on deck and was there
most of the night. The next morning she looked
very tired when she muttered, 'what will become
of us.' We replied, 'Don't worry Mum we'll be
all right.' That cheered her up, we all laughed as
usual. The ship turned left or as the Captain said,
to port. The aircraft carrier left us now heading
for Gibraltar. Our ship continued to zigzag down
the African coast. The Blitz kid and I continued
to take our turns on the Bridge. The sea was a
different colour now and the waves much bigger.
The Captain told us to keep our eyes skinned as
U-boats still operate out of French ports.

I was losing all sense of time, I think it was
the forth day out from Gibraltar that the women

on deck started screaming, U-boat, U-boat. 'Not again,' said an agitated Captain, 'get those women below deck Mr. Trimble.' 'Aye, Aye sir.' Mr. Trimble rushed down the steps shouting, 'get below, you lot.'

This time the Captain looked worried, 'can you see anything?' he asked. We looked in the direction the women were pointing. It was very hard to tell because of the big waves and many of them had white tops which made it even more difficult. The kid wasn't sure but he thought he saw something different in a wave pattern. It was a long way out, he reported it to the Captain. 'I can't see anything, here kid use my binoculars.' We waited, 'yes there it is, just as you showed us with your pipe.' 'Mr. Trimble radio to the Destroyers suspected sub on our starboard side.' Mr. Trimble disappeared to the radio room. 'What's gone wrong this time,' the Captain was pacing up and down, 'they have radar which can pick a submarine on the surface and they have asdic for underwater.' The Destroyers obviously picked up something as they sent off depth charges which exploded with unbelievable force. This must have gone on for some time as we could still hear the explosions going on long after we had passed. The radio crackled, Mr. Trimble returned, 'All clear now sir, apologies from the Commodore, Destroyers. Sorry, our fault it will not happen again. End message.'

That lovely smell again of the Captain's pipe filled the Bridge. He must be relaxed. 'Well now, I didn't believe those women and I still don't think they saw the sub, it was just coincidence, call it luck, that you saw the sub just in time. That calls for another celebration, let's break open some Hershey bars. The kid and I finished our shift on the Bridge and returned below deck.

CHAPTER 12

Late April 1944 – The Atlantic

Time seemed to stand still, the days came and went and the sea changed to a sort of rolling motion at least the sun was shining. We continued with our watch on the Bridge. The kid was always asking where are we now and when will we get to this place called Liverpool. The Captain didn't mind in fact he told Mr. Trimble that we were great company, Mr Trimble agreed. They took it in turns to show us where we are, which was in mid Atlantic somewhere. That meant in a few days time we would see Northern Ireland and then down the Irish Sea to Liverpool. Mum used to see us on the Bridge and waved, she seemed happy enough just knowing we were happy in having a job to do.

Once Northern Ireland came into view we noticed a change in Mum. She mentioned Dad a few times wondering where he was. It was over a year since we saw him. There was always one thing she never doubted, he is alive somewhere.

All the escort vessels disappeared and there
it was Liverpool at last. The Captain and Mr.
Trimble were very busy getting the ship into dock
with the aid of Tugs.

Mum got our things ready. We went to see the
Captain as soon as the ship tied up. 'Ready to
disembark, all ship shape and Bristol fashion. Mr
Trimble and I will miss you very much. We saved a
treat for you, two Hershey bars.' With that he and
Mr. Trimble gave us a cuddle. The blitz kid cried
and I didn't wag my tail.

Mum could see we were upset as we walked
down to the dockside, she didn't say anything.
The whole dock was teeming with people, mostly
sailors and troops. They all seemed to be going
our way, which was towards a sign saying taxi. We
lined up and waited and moved a bit and waited
then a bit more and waited. Taxis were flying in
and out taking people to an unknown destination.
The kid and I spoke to each other, have you
noticed that these soldiers and sailors have bellies.
They must be receiving food on a regular basis.
Not like Malta at all. Have you noticed something
else, I said. No what's that, said the kid. Look up
there, urrh what's that, we both said. Go on then
ask Mum. 'Mum what's that up there.' 'What's
what?' Oh that grey stuff you mean, you'll get used
to it.' We both spoke again, does that mean we

will never see the sun again. 'Of course you will,
this not like Malta, sometimes it can take days,
eventually the sun will shine again.' We moved
a bit more still looking around. It stinks of black
stuff like those ships that were sunk in Malta.
Look at those metal things in the ground what do
they do, ask Mum. 'What are those things in the
ground,' the kid was pointing at them. 'That's for a
train, you'll soon see because we will be travelling
on one to go to Glasgow.'

Eventually we reached the front of the line and
a taxi pulled up. The taxi driver shouted at Mum.
'Where are you going to Missus.' Glasgow.' The taxi
driver looked at us, then he turned his attention to
someone behind us. It was a sailor with two others
and the sailor was waving money. 'Not you Missus,
said the driver, get in you lot.' They did and he was
gone. So much for big brave men here in England,
not like Malta at all. Again we waited until at last
a taxi came that would take us to the train.

Mum got the tickets and we stood on a platform
along with hundreds of troops until a train came
in. Nobody helped us and we struggled on board.
It was packed, there were no seats and so the
kid and I sat on the suitcase. Mum had to push
and shove to find a space in the corridor for the
suitcase. The train slowly started to move. The kid
and I couldn't move and Mum was doing her best

to keep soldiers away from us. They all seemed to smoke and they all smelled. I wondered if any of them had ever been under fire. I doubted it they all talked too loudly and they had full bellies. Mum was left standing and protecting us. After a while there was a commotion along the corridor. A man was telling the soldiers to move out of his way. It was an officer, he soon reached us and stopped. Looking at Mum and us he said, 'is this your kid and his companion.' Mum gave a simple reply, 'yes.' The officer wore a red cap and carried a side arm. 'Right,' he looked very angry, his face almost the same colour as his cap. 'Wait a minute,' and with that he went into a compartment. We heard him talking loudly, 'you must know there is a lady out here with a kid and his companion and you lot sitting comfortably. Get out now, just wait until you see some action, perhaps you'll learn how to behave after that.' He came back to us, 'I am sorry Madam, they just don't know how to behave. You will travel in comfort and quiet for the rest of the journey.' We all thanked him very much, I heard him muttering to himself as he walked away, I could have sworn the kid and the dog said something.

CHAPTER 13

Glasgow

The train rumbled on and on very slowly. It stopped frequently and the soldiers diminished in numbers. The guard came along and poked his head into the compartment, 'Glasgow next stop.' Mum looked relieved, 'thank goodness, we can get our things into the suitcase for the last time.' It was cold and dark when we left the train. Walking along the platform we came to a big area where there were just a few people looking up at a notice board with nothing on it. There was a railwayman telling the people no more trains tonight. Mum didn't want a train she wanted a taxi. She told us to sit on the suitcase while she went and found one. After a few minutes she was back, 'there are none, looks like we will be here all night.' I noticed a man with gold braid on his cap he was looking at us for some time before approaching. 'You seem to be in trouble, where exactly are you going.' Mum replied, 'I'm trying to get to my mother-in-law in Knightswood but there are no taxis.' The man had a kindly face he said, 'wait here, it may take me some time, I think I know where there will be a taxi.' He was as good as his word, returning after a while with a taxi. 'I've told the driver where you want to go, so in you get. I wish you well.'

'Mum what is a mother-in law,' asked the kid. ' You and Stupid must call her Granny, she is Dad's mother.' We both said together, where is Dad. There were tears in her eyes before she spoke, 'I just don't know, now you two don't let Granny hear you talking together yet. Let her get used to the idea that you communicate to one another, here we are.' With that the taxi pulled up outside a house. We couldn't see much being so dark. There were two doors, Mum knocked on one. Someone came down stairs, it was this person called Granny. 'Well hello,' she said, 'I was expecting you, come upstairs.' How was she expecting us, the kid and I wondered. Mum couldn't have told her, I guess we'll find out later, she continued, 'You must be very tired I've prepared the bedroom for you, so get some sleep and let's talk in the morning.'

CHAPTER 14

May 1944

Early next morning the kid and I looked around
the place. There were two bedrooms a kitchen
and one living room. Granny was already up and
preparing breakfast, porridge she said it was.
This is for you Stupid, I know exactly what you
need because of Bunty and Rose. The kid and
I looked at each other, who on earth are Bunty
and Rose. We were careful not to start chatting
to each other. Anyway thanks to Bunty and Rose
it was a jolly good breakfast. Mum joined us and
immediately began chatting to Granny, getting
up to date on matters. The important issue as far
we all were concerned is how did Granny know
we were coming. Mum posed the question and
Granny answered, 'I had a telegram two days ago,
telling me to expect you.' 'Who sent the telegram,'
asked the kid.' 'Why it was your Dad of course.' So
he was alive after all, Mum always knew he would
be. That meant he knew all the time where we
were, which also meant we would never find out
until the end of this war where he is.

Mum had to go out with Granny for something
called ration books. This was necessary for us to
get food and all things we needed to live. It was
cold in Glasgow and the kid needed extra clothes.
I was okay with all my thick fur I soon got used
to the cold. Mum told us to go and explore, so
off we went. We soon met two kids in the street,
Tommy and Maureen, they were to become good
friends. They took us up the street to a shop called
McGregors. It was a sweet shop but the chances of
getting any chocolate without a ration book were
nil. Even with a ration book it was useless, because
it wasn't real chocolate like Hersheys.

The Blitz Kid and I decided to have a council of
war. There was a hill behind Granny's place, we
climbed it in order to be alone so we could talk
things over. Firstly the chocolate game has ended
most probably until the end of the war. People do
have full bellies though, but they are full of stuff
like porridge, cabbage, potatoes and bits of meat.
Mind you Granny does make one thing which
is excellent, spotted dick. I can share in some of
that, it really fills us up. Scotland was starting
to be a problem with our health, it was cold and
wet. Mum is very thin and she has a problem with
her teeth. The Blitz Kid is looking none too good,
always having a cold or something. I was bearing
up but feeling that a lot had been taken out of me.

It was the army doctors that told Mum she had a gum disease and the kid had suffered malnutrition. Malta was the cause and now the Scottish climate put paid to it all. Mum lost all her teeth, she looked good with a full set of dentals but still very thin. The kid had his tonsils out, there didn't seem to be much improvement afterwards. We were being looked after by the army for our health needs. The doctors advised that we go abroad or as far south as possible after the war.

The good news is we have great new friends in Tommy and Maureen. We used to go up to the canal and watch the horses pull the barges and on one occasion an MTB came through very slowly. We loved the noise of the engines. Of course what was even better there was no enemy aircraft trying to kill us. Dad's sister, auntie Queenie lived nearby with uncle Sherry and cousins Dick and Billy. Dick being older didn't play with us but Billy did. Maureen was a little so and so, tearing around all over the place even though she had leg irons, polio they said it was. Whilst playing one day she gave the kid a wallop on the head with a dustbin lid. It left him with a great scar.

CHAPTER 15

End of May beginning of June 1944

Granny said why we didn't get any letters from Dad was because if the enemy got hold of one they would then know where he was and put two and two together finding out what he was doing. The telegram she received came directly from army HQ.

It was a sunny and warm day for a change and we were playing with Tommy and Maureen as usual in the street. I sensed something was up and warned the kid.

The two of us stopped playing, it wasn't like an air raid coming, we could always sense them before the sirens started, no, this felt good. There in the distance was a soldier approaching with a kit bag over his shoulder. We couldn't be sure at first, then we were, we ran shouting and me barking DAD. The kit bag was dropped and we ran into his arms. Oh, what joy to feel and see him again that lovely smell of Dad he was with us and all felt good.

You can imagine how Mum felt, she always had faith he was alive and here he was. The tears of sheer joy came from all of us even Granny cried.

'Are you here for good now?' It was the kid expressing all our thoughts into words. 'No, only two weeks,' said Dad quietly.' Mum nearly fainted she looked very weak. 'Only two weeks, you've been away from us all this time and the army can only give you just two weeks.' Dad held her in his arms, 'I can't tell you why, there is something big on, Granny will no doubt read all about it in good time. Anyway let's look in my kit bag and see what I have. Firstly Mum and Stupid, I am afraid all I have is a few handkerchiefs and some dried bones. For the kid there are these toys the troops made.' They were magnificent wooden models of aeroplanes all painted in their camouflage colours, beautiful.

The next two weeks were fantastic, we lived as a family again. Going for long walks, going for bus rides to Loch Lomond and we especially enjoyed going on the tram cars to Glasgow. It ended all too soon and Dad packed his kit bag said his cheerio and was gone. We wondered when we would see him again.

There was one bit of good news, a parcel arrived from uncle Pat in New York, America. It must have been Granny who said we had arrived in

Scotland. When opened it contained all sorts of goodies not available in Great Britain and guess what else, Hershey bars of chocolate. These parcels arrived on a regular basis and followed our every move for years to come. They were a much needed addition to our diet for the recovery from Malta. At Christmas and every Christmas for many years to come there came a beautiful tin in which was a Christmas cake. Our friends and family shared in the cake. Thanks to uncle Les, of Denver stores, Brooklyn America. Not only that there was another parcel from Eire, Southern Ireland. Sent by uncle Henry it contained lovely Irish butter. We were rich indeed.

Granny had a special chair in which she sat and read the daily paper. The news came of the invasion, It was called 'D' day, 6th of June 1944. She always called Mum in from the kitchen and read what was happening. Mum, the kid and I would sit in a chair behind her and watch the reading. All the words were pointed out with her finger. I suppose this was to help Mum learn about reading. For days and then weeks of listening and then watching the finger, the kid said he could read.

CHAPTER 16

June/July 1944

Everyday after breakfast, Granny would sit in
her chair and read the newspaper. The headlines
always carried the news of how the invasion was
proceeding. Mum came in from the kitchen
everyday to listen and the kid would learn
even more. If only we knew where Dad was, it
amounted to guess work. Whenever the Engineers
were mentioned making a bridge or whatever,
our hearts jumped at the thought it may be him.
Granny said the news from the South of England
wasn't good with things called doodlebugs going
off and then another thing called a V2. These
were rockets which blew up on landing causing
massive damage. Mum's sister lives in Surrey
which is near London. Auntie as we call her, with
her two boys, Armando and Mario were evacuated
from Gibraltar when there was fear of invasion
by German and Spanish forces. They first went
to Casablanca, under the protection of French
forces. With the capitulation of France they were
in danger of being sent to a concentration camp.

Especially as Auntie's husband was a nurse looking after the insane from Gibraltar. So British forces swiftly moved them to Surrey, England, which although it had the threat of bombing, was better than the concentration camp.

Our health improved, with the kid and I enjoying a peaceful life without bombing. Mum was more of a worry she still looks thin and washed out. Although she doesn't say, 'what will become of us,' any more, we knew Dad was always in her thoughts.

Mr. and Mrs. Woodhouse with their daughter Nan lived below us. Mum and Mrs. Woodhouse were always chatting. Mr. Woodhouse was a post office engineer, being a reserved occupation he wasn't in the forces. He had a garden shed in which he used to make things out of wood. We loved to watch him make things in the shed especially as he smoked a pipe. It reminded us of being on board the ship with the Captain and Mr. Trimble. We could never forget that lovely smell.

'Mr. Woodhouse,' it was the kid talking, 'who are Bunty and Rose, Granny is always talking about them and looking at Stupid at the same time.' Mr. Woodhouse loaded his pipe and lit it before answering. 'They were dogs, two Pekinese and your Granny was very fond of them. They died a few years ago, although they were old your Granny

114

never got over their deaths and I guess that is why she remembers them when looking at Stupid.' That explains a lot, I said to the kid. 'Thanks Mr. Woodhouse.' He looked at us and smiled. We didn't see Nan standing behind us looking thoughtful, 'coming for a walk, to the Co-op?' Nan was much older than the kid, we must be careful I think she knows we communicate.

CHAPTER 17

August to September 1944

We joined a bunch of kids getting up to all sorts of mischief, it was a shame Maureen couldn't join in owing to her leg irons. She certainly made up for it at other times when we played in the street. We often felt the wallop of anything that came to hand from her. The kid was paid for this misbehaviour, when climbing over a fence, with a rusty nail ripping through his leg. Granny took charge when this sort of thing happened by way of a complete strip of clothes and standing in a wash tub with a scrub down. I watched her carefully whenever this happened, there, unbeknown to the kid, she always tried not to laugh. The mark the nail left, healed on its own, leaving a beautiful scar to be proud of for life. That made two with the dustbin lid gift from Maureen. There was always weddings to attend. This was a regular feature in war time with a member of the forces marrying a sweetheart before being sent abroad. A bunch of us always got the message and off we rushed just in time to catch the couple leaving the chapel. We gave them a good send off, in the hope that when they threw coins in the air there would be a few bawbees as well as pennies.

Life was good, we had full bellies and the food parcels from America always arrived, with chocolate of course. Uncle Pat also sent a roll of New York newspapers including the comic section on a regular basis. I used to sit with the kid looking at the life everybody in America was living, it was our dream, maybe someday, just maybe.

At the end of September Mum paid a visit to the army doctors. She came back with a surprise, she was pregnant. Granny was pleased but worried, Mum was still recovering from Malta. The kid and I knew if Mum could survive Malta she would come through anything. Dad needed to be informed, he was sure to be delighted. The baby was due to be born sometime in March 1945. Well that's funny I thought, it's the same month as the kid's birthday. Granny wrote to the army. They made sure he received the good news. Will Dad be allowed to come home, we knew he wasn't allowed to write to us, perhaps he will turn up one day.

CHAPTER 18

October to December 1944

'Mum Mr. Woodhouse says he will make some toys for us once he knows whether it's a boy or a girl.' 'I suppose you and Stupid have been down there in his shed bothering him again.' 'No we haven't, have we Stupid, he likes us there, it keeps him company, he says.' Mum thought for a bit. 'It's that pipe of his, just like the Captain with his pipe, you love the smell, I know.' We will be careful we both said together, in doggy. 'Don't let your Granny see you talking together.' We won't Mum.

Everyday Granny read to us the newspaper, pointing as usual with her finger each word for Mum to learn. She didn't realise that the kid was learning as well.

We had to guess where Dad was by following the war in Europe. It seemed to be going well with the enemy falling back through France and Belgium. Granny read to us about the fighting in other parts of the world. That seemed to be going okay as well. Looks like we will win after all, which is a totally different picture from Malta just a short while ago.

Tommy and Maureen were getting excited about a thing called Halloween. We didn't understand until Granny told us the kids get dressed up in funny clothes and come around knocking on doors shouting, 'trick or treat'. On Halloween night Granny prepared a big bowl of apples bobbing in water. The kid and I had great fun watching them bobbing for an apple. If they got one, that was the treat. There were no sweeties, the war put paid to that. The days were getting shorter, no sooner was it light than it seemed to start getting dark and colder much colder. We were told to expect snow soon. This should be fun, Tommy told us about sledging on the hill behind Granny's place.

It was near Christmas and Mum was looking much better. I could hear her talking to Mrs. Woodhouse downstairs and laughing a lot. Christmas in Scotland was a brief celebration of just one day. New year's eve, hogmanay and new year's day being celebrated more than Christmas. This was our first Christmas without the threat of being blown to bits or drowned. Without Dad it felt, well, sort of empty. So we got on with it knowing Dad would be with us for many Christmases to come. The food was just plain

119

stomach filling stuff. The difference compared
to most people, was uncle Pat's food parcel with
chocolate and uncle Les's Christmas cake, both or
which arrived just in time for the celebration.

The war news was alarming, Granny read to us
the story of the enemy almost breaking through
our lines over Christmas. Heavy fighting took
place in snowy weather before they were stopped.
It was snowing at home as well, this being our first
experience of what fun it could be. All the kids,
except poor Maureen of course, were sledging
down the hill behind Granny. That included
the kid and I. Inevitably the snow melted and
we played in the street again. It was then that
Maureen certainly made us pay for deserting her
by chasing us and giving a wallop with anything
handy. She could really move on the flat despite
the leg irons.

CHAPTER 19

January to March 1945

Mum continued to be well and putting on weight. The kid was always asking is the baby coming yet and am I going to have a brother or a sister. Mum became really fed up with this and eventually stopped him by saying that the next parcel from America, even if had chocolate in it he wouldn't be getting any. That would mean me as well so I made sure not another word was spoken about the baby until he or she arrived.

Granny used to take us to Glasgow on the Tram. The new Trams as she called them were too high for her to climb into. So we had to look out and be prepared to say, not this one Granny, sometimes we had to wait ages before the right Tram came along. In Glasgow we used to wait outside the shops whilst she got what was needed. We noticed baby clothes being on the shopping list more and more. There was a noise, a very loud noise, like a clickerty clacking echoing round the buildings. It had a rhythm to it, what was it? Granny took us from whence it came. It was a group of boys, a gang if you like and the noise came from clogs. They were very disciplined to produce a rhythmic sound, scary for some. Compared with bombing it was kids play, literally.

Mum was going to see the doctors and nurses on a regular basis at a Nursing Home, checking that everything was okay with her health. It was on the 17th of March that an army ambulance was called by Tommy's mum who had a telephone and off Mum went to the Nursing Home. Now that is really funny I thought, one day before the Blitz kid's birthday.

18th March 1945 Happy birthday kid, I said the next morning. Tommy's mum came rushing across the road and up the stairs to see Granny. 'It's a boy,' she said. Granny nearly choked on her toast, 'how are they both?' 'Very well indeed, and you will be able to visit them this afternoon.'

I spoke to the kid, what a birthday present, a brother. 'Does that mean Stupid and I can visit him as well?' 'No,' answered Granny, 'I have arranged for auntie Cathy to come and stay here for a few days until Mum can cope with everything.' You will remember Dad having two brothers in the navy, both on Battleships. Well one was married to auntie Cathy who will be looking after us whilst Mum is away. Cathy was the greatest cook ever, her scones were simply the best. After about three days auntie took us along to see our new brother. We weren't allowed in to the nursing home only to look at him through the window.

There he was with Mum holding him up at the window. The kid smiled, I wagged my tail. 'He hasn't any hair, has he auntie.' 'Yes he has,' replied auntie, 'it's very fair that's all.' We had to wait outside whilst auntie went in and had a good look and no doubt gave the new kid a cuddle. A discussion took place between us, what shall we call him. He looked sort of round to me, I said. Yes and if his hair is going to stay that colour very blond. He cannot be called blitz kid two, there is no blitz here. Our brother has got big ears and a round head. Definitely cannot call him big ears but we can call him the Scots Kid. We agreed that was it the Scots Kid.

Going home with auntie we felt very pleased with ourselves. A few days later the Scots Kid arrived home with Mum. A gathering took place welcoming them home, Mrs. Woodhouse, Tommy's mum, two aunties and Granny. What a fuss they made of the new kid. I bit Mum on the big toe. She hit the roof, 'why on earth did you do that, Stupid?' The Ladies looked at each other and they said together, you paid too much attention to David. 'Oh! of course,' said Mum, 'I'm sorry you two, it won't happen again.'

123

CHAPTER 20

April to May 1945

'David is that going to be the name of our brother,' asked the kid of Mum. 'Yes Dad and I agreed before he went away, that if I became pregnant and had a boy he would be called David. What do you two think?' It's okay, we both said together. Granny continued to read the newspaper everyday with Mum the kid and I sitting behind her. The kid was learning all the time it won't be long before he surprises everyone with his reading. The war seems to be progressing well. Dad must be coming home soon. He knows about David because Granny wrote to Dad through the army, Giving all the details of David.

8th of May 1945 and Granny was very excited, the war was over. There are celebrations taking place everywhere. We helped Granny put up flags along the windowsill.

How come these people are celebrating victory when our Dad is still out there somewhere. It seems to me that the real heroes aren't here they

are either dead or still doing their job. Anyway
Granny says there is still a war to be won against
the Japanese. So where is our Dad will he now go
and fight the Japanese.

A letter arrived from Dad, he could now write to
us. He will not be able to get away until August or
September. Mum was very upset saying what more
do the army want Dad completed his 21 years of
service and the extra 6 years because of the war
and it is another 3 or 4 months before he is free. It
just didn't seem fair.

Granny announced that she was going to visit
uncle Henry in Bray, Co. Wicklow, Eire. And she
was going to fly there. Civilian flying from Renfrew
had restarted. In a few days she would be off.

The next morning after the announcement, the
Blitz kid was sitting in Granny's chair, the one she
always sat in to read the newspaper. He had the
paper open and was reading something. I quietly
barked, you're in trouble. 'Get out now!' No I won't,
was the reply. 'Get out now and stop pretending
to read the newspaper.' I'm not pretending to read
the newspaper, I am reading it.' 'Oh you are, are
you, well read me something.' So the kid did and
he used his finger over each word, just like Granny.
She stood muttering something and then called
Mum. 'Go on show your mother what you can do.'
Mum watched the kid run his finger over every

125

word reading out loud. 'We've got you to thank for that Granny, all these months you have been showing me how to read and he has picked it up perfectly.'

Granny said thoughtfully, 'I think I will buy him some books before I go to Eire. We needn't tell anyone about this, let them find out when he goes to school.' I could see Granny change when she said that. She was proud and I saw a twinkle in her eye.

CHAPTER 21

June to July 1945

Granny packed her bag, which was quite small, just enough for a few days. We made arrangements to meet her at the airport on her return. It would be good to be around 'planes again. We were thinking of George and all our friends who helped save our lives. The taxi came and off she went.

So what are we going to do now, Mum will be busy with David, let's go and find Maureen and Tommy. We searched everywhere without success. Walking up the street was Tommy's mum, where are they. At school she said. Both of our friends are older than the kid and it was time for school.

'Come on Stupid we are going to find them.' Off we went, the school is at the end of the road. The gate needed pushing and in we went. The front door was heavy but we managed to open it just enough to squeeze in. Along the corridor there were lots of doors to class rooms. We had to jump to see in each one. At the third attempt we saw Maureen in the back of a class. The kid went in, the teacher was surprised, 'what can I do for you

and the dog,' she said. The kid answered without
hesitation, 'we want to join and this is Stupid,
he's called that because he's not.' The teacher was
even more surprised. 'What do you mean, 'join',
this isn't a club, this is a school and definitely not
for dogs.' She tried to show them the door but the
kid was determined. 'We used to play in the street
together now Maureen and Tommy are no longer
there, they are here.' He said pointing at the two
friends. 'They are here are because they are older
than you,' she said looking at the kid and Stupid.
It was the kid again, 'well I still want to join with
Stupid.' The teacher didn't know what to say she
obviously hadn't been confronted with a situation
like this before, she thought for a second. 'Come
with me, both of you. Class! look at some books
until I return and keep quiet.

We marched along the corridor to a room
marked 'Headmistress'. We waited outside until
a voice said, 'come in, well now what do we have
here.' The Teacher had told the Headmistress
about us, so she immediately said, 'does your
Mother know you are here.' The kid and I shook
our heads. 'I thought so, if you go home now and
come back with some sandwiches for lunch which
your mother has packed for you, you can stay for
the morning. You can tell her that I must see her
first thing tomorrow morning. One thing, no dogs.'

I heard her say to the Teacher as we left, do you know I could have sworn that dog understood every word I said and he shook his head in answer to my question.

Mum laughed a lot as she packed the lunch she even made one up for me. I simply waited on the doorstep until the kid finished school. The next day Mum saw the Headmistress. She must have told her about us and what we had come through. She also told her that the kid could read and how that came about. However Mum told me that there was no change of heart when it came to me. Well not yet anyway. So that was it then the kid went to school in the mornings and I went with him staying on the school doorstep. The Headmistress watched all the children making a fuss of me everyday and me being so well behaved. One day it was pouring with rain she invited me in and said, 'I think you understand everything I say, so if I let you stay with the Blitz Kid', Mum must have told her, 'I expect you to behave at all times, is that a deal.' She watched me very carefully and very closely as I nodded my head. 'I thought so! I thought so, I just knew I was right.' The children soon got used to me in class, I became just another kid.

Auntie Queenie heard from Granny she was coming home from Eire. We went to meet her with our cousin Billy. It was a lovely afternoon at

Renfrew airport, watching the aircraft, hoping to see some fighters and perhaps George. It wasn't to be all we saw were yellow biplanes. One landed near us and without stopping the engine came towards us waiting just outside a hangar. The pilot ran straight into the hanger until the propeller hit the wall smashing it to pieces which stopped the engine. Out the pilot jumped and walked by us with a wave saying what do think of that one then.

Granny arrived in a biplane, it had 12 wicker seats the colour was silver and blue. The Pilot reminded us of our friends in Malta, he was ever so nice. It must be being close to death that teaches us how to treat others. He took the kid, placed him in the pilots seat and started the engines.

CHAPTER 22

August to September 1945

Granny was home but where was Dad? Mum was going to the clinic with David, sometimes he didn't look too good. The army doctors wanted to see the kid with Mum and David and when they did it wasn't good news. They told Mum when your husband gets here you must move as far south as possible or to a warm place abroad, if you want your two boys to survive.

It was the summer holidays and now all the kids returned to having fun during the long daylight hours. David our brother seemed cheerful enough and we hoped the army doctors would prove to be wrong.

Soon it will be September, the end of the school holidays and still no Dad. Then one day we were playing with Tommy and Maureen as usual when I could sense a different atmosphere. I asked the kid if he had noticed anything different. 'Not really,' he said, 'I'm continually trying to keep out of

Maureen's way. If she gets me I will be clobbered again.' Come on let's walk down the street together on our own, you may feel something then.

When on our own we sat down and listened, nothing. Wait a minute I can hear footsteps, army boots it must be Dad. We stood up and ran towards the sound and there he was, Dad.

Home for good this time, we danced around him as he walked along. The first thing he asked was is Mum okay and how is David. Just great we said you'll see. Mum was in tears with happiness. Dad held David he looked at the little fellow and smiled. So this was it our little family together forever.

First thing next morning it was time to unpack the kit bag. Right at the top the troops had made extra toys for David and the Blitz Kid. David had a string of beautiful wooden toys to hang up in his pram and the kid another set of model wooden aeroplanes. These toys would keep us occupied for playing on rainy days. Next it was time for Dad to become demobbed, finished with the army forever. He repacked his kit bag and off he went to Glasgow. What a difference on his return, with a new suit, shoes and hat plus a raincoat, he looked smart.

It was time to find a job and Dad had thought about it for some time before leaving the army. It became obvious he wanted nothing more to do

with the army and whatever he did in it. He said to
Mum, 'I'll become a bus driver.' Mum hit the roof,
'you'll do nothing of the sort, after all those years
as an engineer, now you want to be a bus driver.
I want you to go and talk with Mr Woodhouse.'
Dad did, obviously she had been talking to Mr.
Woodhouse who was an engineer working on
telephones in the GPO. The next thing we knew
Dad was taking exams and training to be a
technical officer in the GPO. The army continued
to pay him until trained.

One day all the kids were given a banana, this
issue came from the Government. It being the
one bright moment in the period of continuing
rationing. We had never seen a banana before.
Nan Woodhouse who was much older than the
kid showed him how to peel it. 'Now then,' she
said, 'I am going to the Co-op and when I return,
you will only have eaten it up to here.' She showed
the kid exactly where by peeling up to the place
he should stop. This was to make it last as long as
possible. The trouble was he couldn't stop once
started and he finished it long before she returned.
We hid behind the hedge. I don't think Nan was
surprised not to see us, she knew where we were.
She laughingly shouted out, 'I hope you don't get
tummy ache,' as she entered the house.

The 14th of August 1945, VJ day so the war is

really over at last. Once again Granny put up the flags and that was about it. We didn't feel happy inside, we felt relieved and worn out. Nothing changed, the rationing continued, it even got worse. We won the war, but there was nothing to show for it yet.

At least we are together as a complete family at last and looking forward to a great future. Things are a bit crowded living with Granny. It was Mum who said she would have to do something about that. She was still attending the clinic and worrying about David, although he looked well the doctors knew there was some thing wrong but they didn't know what. It was decided to wait until Dad finished his training as a technical officer on telephones, which would be at Christmas.

CHAPTER 23

October to December 1945

The Blitz Kid and I used to watch the other kids racing around on tricycles. It looked fun and we wanted one. So we asked Dad, he as usual just looked at us. Dad wasn't the same as when we were together in Malta. We could only guess how he was feeling. There were no friends left, Guiseppe had probably gone to Australia, we never heard from him again and Dad never tried to get in touch. Our uncles in America carried on sending the parcels as did our uncle in Eire. To us he was wonderful, everything you could wish for from a Dad. To others he was kind and polite, always helping out when needed. Nobody would ever know his deep innermost feelings. He never forgave the army breaking its promise when we should have been sent to South Africa out of the war zone. He had served for 27 years. 21 of those years under contract, 6 years of war all of which in the front line. Dad had an unblemished record with loads of medals the army said they would send. He told Mum they will be sent back. Mum said we must keep them to pass on to the family.

Christmas 1945. Our first of being a complete family in peace time. Of course we had a roof over our heads, thanks to Granny. We had food although still rationed which helped Granny because we could share some of the rations. The parcels from America arrived on time which included the Christmas cake. Dad did manage to write and thank them for the parcels.

CHAPTER 24

January to April 1946

Dad passed his exams and became a qualified technical officer on British Telephones. He started immediately working in the telephone exchanges around Glasgow. Mum also acted immediately, she told Dad he had to write to her sister in Surrey asking if we could visit. Back came the reply, of course, how about coming when it is warmer in April. That is it then, April we visit Auntie in Surrey, England.

One day Dad said to the kid and I, he had seen something we might like in a shop. 'What is it Dad?' the kid was impatient as usual.

'Just wait and see.' We had to catch a tram to the shops and out we jumped. Dad stopped outside a shop marked Bicycles. 'I hope it's still here, these things disappear as soon as they come in.' We looked and there it was a black tricycle. 'Wow is that for us.' It certainly is,' said Dad. As soon as he paid we were off. I climbed on the rear with my paws resting on the kid's shoulders. We didn't get a tram back we cycled all the way with Dad running after us. Mum saw us coming down the road she couldn't believe her eyes as we hurtled towards her. Mobile and free to wander, the next few weeks after school we took off exploring the whole area. Mum would suddenly find us on our tricycle right beside her as she was shopping with David in the pram.

The weeks seemed to flash by as we, the complete family lived as families should. Except of course there was no home of our own. April was approaching and we prepared for the great new adventure of going to England. Dad had given us a book of trains with the Coronation Scot being the one we hoped to be on. It was streamlined and blue with white stripes along the side. The day came, and off we went to the station. There was great excitement when we discovered it was the Coronation Scot. It was a great disappointment, it wasn't blue and it didn't have white stripes down the side. It was black sooty and the stripes were grey sooty. Dad said it was the result of the war. It had never been cleaned for 6 years. We had a sleeping compartment of our own. The kid and I bagged the high bed. It looked comfortable enough but it wasn't. The train kept stopping and starting all night, it meant we were constantly waking up. David seemed okay he slept right through. As we approached London the next day, both sides of the track were piled high with broken aircraft. Nearly all were American, ready for the scrap heap. I knew the kid loved aircraft, we spoke together in doggy, all those beautiful aircraft broken. It was very sad.

London was still showing the signs of a bombed city. Just like Malta although in Malta the buildings were of a light coloured stone and the sun nearly always shone. Here the buildings were dark with soot and the sun shone on and off at least it was on more often than Glasgow and it was warmer. Mum refused to use the escalator to get on the tube, which meant, much to Dad's annoyance, we had to get a taxi across London for the Southern trains. The trains were green and electric. In about 45 minutes we reached our destination. Nobody knew what time we would arrive, so there was nobody to greet us. We walked up this big hill to Auntie's house. Mum hadn't seen her sister since leaving for Malta before the war. Tears of happiness greeted us. Auntie and her family making us most welcome. The family consisted of Auntie, Uncle with two sons, Armando and Mario. Our two cousins were older than us 14 and 8 respectively. That made 8 of us plus me of course squeezed into a small 3 bedroom house. We managed somehow and all got on

139

famously. The idea being we would all live together when moving from Glasgow eventually. Uncle, the psychiatric nurse was still looking after the insane from Gibraltar. As already mentioned their journey to England was hazardous. From Gibraltar to Casablanca and then to England. They all seemed happy enough and settled in England.

We loved this new country, except in trying to get the local kids to understand us. The kid and I had great fun playing in the warmer weather and listening to the different accent. One kid called Robin would run about shouting, dogfight, dogfight, it wasn't dogs fighting it was planes he was talking about. He still thought they were fighting every time he saw them milling about on high. The kid and I knew differently, there was no ratatat of machine guns or any bombs or any black puffs of ack ack guns up in the sky. Sometimes the warm weather felt just like Malta. Which of course Mum wanted for the health of David, the kid and me. There were times when I didn't feel too good.

The return to Scotland took as long as it did coming to England. Mum still refused to use the escalator and the tube across London and the train stop-started all the way.

CHAPTER 25

May to December 1946

Once back in school we became very popular, guess why. Chalk; we noticed that the hill on which Auntie lived was made of chalk and the kid brought back loads of it. In Scotland there was none, it cost money to get some and it was needed to play hop scotch. The kid gave it out to friends especially Tommy and Maureen.

A time was arranged for our return to England and this time it was a one way ticket. We would go back this coming winter December or January 1947. Dad arranged for a transfer to South West London telephone exchanges. Mum continued her visits to the army doctors she told them of the arrangements to go and live in Southern England. They still didn't know what was wrong with David however they thought our best chance of survival was to go south.

Life in Scotland was good the tricycle was our ticket to freedom. The next best thing was ice cream. It came round everyday in the form of an Italian man in a van. The kid and I used to go searching for him on the tricycle listening for the bell, it was always worth it once we found him. Granny always gave us a few pennies for ice cream.

After Mr. Woodhouse knew we would going to Surrey, England he started to make two model buses for David and the kid. The kid and I crowded into his tiny workshop to watch him work. Once again his pipe produced that wonderful smell it even seemed to be in the woodwork of the shed. It reminded us of being back on board the ship with the Captain and Mr. Trimble bound for Liverpool. The buses took months of painstaking work. When it came to the painting, yet another smell welcomed us in the shed. It was the smell of planes just like the paint on spitfires, wonderful. The buses were finally finished in red. Mr. Woodhouse said that was the colour of London buses.

It was November 1946 and we are ready for the move. The days are getting shorter and it is getting cold very cold. There is going to be one more Christmas in Scotland. All is packed ready for moving in January 1947 or so we think. Christmas was great as usual even more so with Dad at home to be Santa. This December was different it was extra cold.

CHAPTER 26

January to May 1947

January came the snow, not ordinary snow,
masses of it, many feet thick. Glasgow came to a
standstill, there were no trams, no buses, no trains
and no school. Food became hard to get, somehow
Dad always managed to get some. It was never as
hard to get as Malta. The cold got us, without coal
we would freeze. The coal was brought upstairs
in a bucket from the bunker. Granny had just
filled the bunker before the bad weather started,
we were lucky. They cut walkways in the middle
of the road for people to walk to work and go to
school. The snow was so deep the kid couldn't see
over the top. Dad said we could stay up late one
night; he took us to the top of the hill behind the
house. He showed us green lights in the sky ever
moving and waving about. It was doubtful, he said,
that we would ever see them again.

Eventually they cleared the snow so that
everything could run again. Months went by
before we could move to England.

May 1947, at last we can move, time to say our goodbyes to all our friends and family. Would we ever see them again, would we ever have a home to call our own? The train couldn't possibly be the Coronation Scot but it was. It wasn't any faster or any cleaner, how many times in the night we were shunted into sidings were uncountable.

When we arrived in London we were exhausted. Across London Mum insisted on a taxi. The red buses are everywhere just like the ones painted by Mr. Woodhouse. All our main baggage like David's pram, the tricycle and the red model buses would arrive later.

Once again we climbed the hill only this time it will need climbing as long as we lived with Auntie.

CHAPTER 27

June to December 1947

We all settled in very well, all 8 of us, well 9 really including me. It was certainly crowded in the tiny house. Mostly happy times followed with the kid and I having as much freedom as in Malta. There would always be one major difference, chocolate. It was still on ration and no troops to get it from. The parcels from America kept coming, which always included chocolate.

The kid went to school in the valley. There was no way of avoiding climbing up and down the hill whichever route you took. A problem arose when the teachers said they couldn't understand a word the kid said. Mum went along to see them, whatever she said it had the right effect because they were very patient after that. I decided not to go to school with the kid. I would stay with Mum and David until after school and we could play in all the fields and woods that are very close. The war had taken its toll on me and I slept a lot of the time. David continued to be a worry for Mum and Dad; still not knowing what was wrong. He rarely played with the other kids, not that he didn't want to he just didn't have the energy.

Dad was enjoying his work, going off to work everyday getting a bus or just walking to whatever telephone exchange. He always walked up the hill in time for tea at 5.30 pm. Mario, went to a different school in the village. Armando being 14 was working as an apprentice engineer.

The summer was gloriously warm and we joined the local gang of kids. We were a wild bunch; most of our Dads had been away fighting the war, some still to return. We rampaged through the countryside like fire literally. As soon as the fields were dry we set light to them, well the kid did anyway. He tried to put it out before leaving. This wasn't always successful so we ran. The Firemen seemed to know who caused the fire and came knocking on our door. Someone had blown the gaff. 'Now look here Missus we are fed up with putting out fires started by your kid. You sort it out and give him a good hiding.' Auntie grabbed the kid and started to wallop him all the way up the hall. Only she didn't, the kid would yelp thinking he was being hit, until he realised he wasn't. This happened twice; the other time was in a war. The wars between our gang and the valleyites were continuous. Valleyites would try and invade our territory, the fields. For us on the hill that was a declaration of war. It was literally sticks and stones. And one well aimed stone caused a problem. A mum turned up on the with her son, 'Look what your kid did to my son.' Well it looked like a pretty good shot to me. He should have ducked, I thought. I must admit the lump on his head was a whopper. 'It just missed his eye,' she continued, 'and I expect you to punish him severely.' Auntie did, in front of the woman, well it looked like it anyway. The kid yelped convincingly and that was that. Scrumping we called it, the nicking of apples from an orchard or garden. This occurred in September when the apples were ripe. The method was to have one of us wearing an over large jumper. He needed to be a good runner and tall, that let the kid out. We lined up on the hedge and two went and surveyed our prey. If the coast was clear over the hedge went the big jumper. The jumper had to be really tight around the waist with a belt. He stuffed the apples down the hole in the neck and bob's yer uncle. It only took a few minutes before he came waddling out. We moved some distance away before divvying them out.

There was one problem, Police Constable England. He was the last outpost of the Metropolitan Police. A one man band on the borders of Surrey police. PC England knew us all and he knew our mums. One day the kid, Billy and me, were doing our scouting bit. Billy is the tall kid who was a good runner . I was acting cavey and the kid was up a tree when I heard PC England coming, he'd spotted us. In his haste to get down the kid got his welly boot stuck. Billy said run, he would get the boot. We ran but PC England was gaining on us. The kid and I spoke in doggy. Let's do the Malta trick I said. 'Okay but don't hurt him.' What with those big police clodhoppers on his feet, no chance. I turned and ran towards this bastion of the law. He hesitated, I bit him on the ankle and ran after the kid. We heard him shouting, 'I know who you two are, The Blitz Kid and Stupid, you wait until I tell your Mum to box your ears.'

He did tell Mum, he showed her the damaged boot, there wasn't a mark on him. I heard Mum tell Auntie that PC England had said if it wasn't for kids like these we would have lost the war. We all loved him and I know he loved us. By the time Christmas came, we were fully at home in Surrey. The kid could be understood at school with the accent quickly disappearing. David was ill, it was strange because he ate very little yet he weighed more than other kids his age. Mum and Dad were happy and looking forward to moving to a home of our own. What little we had in things to make a home arrived from Scotland including the tricycle. Although we all shared everything at Christmas and all the family happy, deep inside there was the thought that next Christmas it would just be the five of us somewhere in a home of our own.

CHAPTER 28

January 1948

The snow and the fog came in January but nothing
like as thick as in Scotland. It was great fun
nevertheless, the gang including Mario our cousin
piled on half an Anderson shelter, it resembled a
great big sledge. Down the fields we went until
coming up against a side of one of the school's air
raid shelters. Then it was up again for another run.
All wars with the valleyites were forgotten in times
of having great fun together. In fact we completely
forgot about time until Dad stood there beside us.
He was furious, when angry he always went very
quiet. We were late for tea and he told Mario to
run home fast. The kid and I walked home with
Dad behind us. The ground is very steep and going
uphill Dad slipped all over the place. He tried to
punish us by giving a hefty kick up the backside.
Missed, he went tumbling down the hill, we ran
home and told Mum. All three of us couldn't stop
laughing. Even when Dad arrived he had to join in
laughing. Mario wasn't so lucky, he got the belt, a
big fat leather belt.

Word came we were offered a council house or rather the upstairs part of a house. It was called a requisitioned house after the army had taken it over as part of the defence for a railway line. It was in a very posh road, very quiet with a lawn tennis club opposite us.

Heaven at last, walks in woods and recreation grounds. Fishing for newts and frogs, watching trains puffing by and long bus rides into the country.

Our family was settled into a home of our own and although not a complete house we had a front door and a garden which we called ours. They found out what was wrong with David. He was sent off to Great Ormond Street Hospital. Mum and Dad used to visit him there. His chance of survival improved greatly.

I was very tired and I knew the time was approaching to say goodbye.

The kid and I laid on the grass, lying in the warm sunshine, talking doggy. I wanted him to remember everything I did since joining the family as a puppy. I wanted him to write it all down so that one day you all would see the result. This is it.

Goodbye The Blitz Kid, until we meet again, it was good.

DAD

What happened to Dad after he left us in Malta? I knew it would be an incomplete story. Like so many men caught up in war they were reluctant to talk about just what did happen.

First a few facts about Malta.

- Population at the beginning of the war... 270,000

- Malta, tonnes of bombs dropped for the whole of the war ie 1940/43... 15,000

- London, tonnes of bombs dropped for the whole of the war... 18,291

- Malta, number of air raids 1940/43... 3343

- Malta, tonnes of bombs for the month of April 1942... 6,728.

- Dresden, tonnes of bombs... 3,900

- Coventry, tonnes of bombs... 818

The following notes are compiled from the few times Dad spoke to me about events after leaving Malta in 1943.

P.L.U.T.O. – Pipeline Under The Ocean

Dad always described his work in the army from 1943 to the end of the war May 1945 as being secret. This gave him the excuse of saying as little as possible about PLUTO. He had no problem in telling us that he worked on PLUTO and that it started from the Isle of Wight.

Remember, we as a family had been in the front line in Malta. For example, the Germans had made Imtarfa hospital a focal point in bombing Takali airfield. I met a wonderful man, a Spitfire reconnaissance pilot who was returning on the 20th of March 1942 from a mission. He watched the Germans lining up on the red cross for their bombing run. I saw the red cross, it was still there in the 1970s, it was massive. I would judge it to be 30 to 40 feet across. The Germans purposely bombed the hospital even though they knew it contained many of their own and Italian airmen.

Dad always felt the army had broken its word when it promised to move us out of the war zone after the siege was lifted. He was always very bitter about this broken promise to the end of his days. Despite those feelings Dad carried out his orders in full earning many medals for exemplary work.

PLUTO is described as WWII's greatest secret.

General Eisenhower said, 'second in daring only to the artificial Mulberry harbours.'

Lord Mountbatten originated the idea of PLUTO. It became the world's first underwater oil pipeline.

Dad was an expert in cabling hence he was needed for PLUTO. The pipeline itself was a flexible pipe made in the same manner as a cable. It was mounted on a 30 ft diameter drum which turned as the ship moved through the water unravelling the pipeline.

After many years of questioning Dad where had he landed on D-day he eventually told me, when I was about 18 years old, Arromanches. Who did you land with I asked, the Marines, he said and that was it.

_____

It was many years later that my wife and I decided to visit the Normandy landing beaches. Dad had died and I was interested in seeing where he actually landed. We visited the Arromanches war museum where they showed a movie of the actual landing. Dad always said the engineer's motto was, in first and out last. True to his word we saw the combat engineers coming in first with the job of removing all mines from the beach obstacles before the infantry could land. So where was Dad I asked the lady in charge of the museum. She in turn asked me what was his job and I mentioned PLUTO. Ah no, she said he didn't land here he landed 14 kilometers towards the American beaches a place called Port en Bessin. So off we went, the lady had told us to go slowly as it was easy to miss.

D-day + 2 Dad was unravelling the pipeline from the drum off the Normandy coast at Port en Bessin.

D-day + 6 approximately, Dad landed at Port en Bessin. Where was Gerry at that time in that particular place, about 200 to 300 hundred yards inland.

My wife and I were driving down a road to Port en Bessin. Coming from Arromanches we turned right following the sign. It was a narrow and steep road twisting and turning its way to the Port. On the way down I had the feeling that Dad had been here.

From earliest childhood I was taught many things of an engineering nature. How to mix various strengths of concrete and mortar, depending on the job in hand. How to provide a good base for heavy road traffic to a footpath. How to reinforce the work with various metals. Right down to very small work with a soldering iron. Making a one valve radio at 10 years old. All these things that Dad taught me came in useful later in life.

As we slowly proceeded down towards the Port, I noticed metal and concrete works going up the steep hill. Works that were designed to carry pipes. I knew immediately, that is my Dad's work.

Well here we are in Port en Bessin and there's a monument to PLUTO. Where are we exactly. The

Allies said they didn't have a port until Cherbourg became available. Which was sometime after D-day. There is still much evidence of PLUTO landing here and this is a port isn't it? They simply lied; there was no way Gerry would ever find out that Gasoline was being pumped right under their noses to our front line. As it is said, it was the best kept secret of WWII.

Standing on the dockside and looking inland we can get our bearings quite easily. To our left are the beaches of the Canadian and British forces, Juno and Gold. To our right are the American beaches, Omaha and Utah. And here we are the port that doesn't exist even to day in most history books. When did you see a movie telling what is most probably the winning ace in the war, PLUTO. Imagine Gasoline pumped right to the frontline and nobody seemed to know how.

Meanwhile the German E-boats and some U-boats where waiting in Le Havre, Boulogne and Cherbourg for the juicy targets of oil tankers. They would have stopped the invasion point blank.

There simply were none.

At a small tourist office we asked if here was any photos of PLUTO landing. Yes of course and you are in luck they are in the Mayor's office which is open this afternoon for an exhibition of paintings. We found the Mayor's office empty except for a young lady on the telephone. When she eventually finished I asked if we could see the photos of PLUTO. We were told, they are displayed on both sides of the corridor leading to the Mayor's office.

There they were and there was Dad and who is with him in the photos, the Marines of course.

On arriving home I told Mum of what we found at Port en Bessin. Her reaction in words was quite simple, 'I'm not surprised.'

In all those miles through France, Belgium, Holland and Germany I can only recall Dad telling me of three incidents and one observation.

In a field somewhere Dad set up a new pumping station. Whilst working he noticed troops a couple of fields away working on what looked like a clearing up job. They both waved cheerfully to each other. That evening, they couldn't work at night for obvious reasons, the CO asked wee Jock as he was known, his map co-ordinates for the end of that day. The CO asked if he was sure, yes absolutely he was told. The CO disappeared, obviously checking with an intelligence Officer. When he returned he asked Dad if he had seen any troop movements. Oh yes he was told, we waved to each other. The CO said, you were in front of the front line as those were Gerrys. Dad knew that and he also knew they were German engineers clearing up after their troops. In first out last, both sides too busy with their work to worry about friend or foe.

It was in Belgium and he was walking into a town with some of his men. Just past a cross roads in the town centre, with people milling about and a Policeman on duty. He felt something and looked round, there was nothing there, all gone, the policeman, people, buildings the lot. Then came the noise. It was a V2.

Dad noticed an increase in civilian traffic everywhere he went in Belgium. You can guess what was happening.

I asked Dad why did Gerry lose the war, he said one word, oil.

Dad liked Belgium, he thought they were marvellous at creating art work from concrete. Only an engineer could think like that.

God bless you Dad I'm really looking forward to meeting you again.

STUPID!

21809454R00090

Printed in Great Britain
by Amazon